COOKERY INTERNATIONAL

SPECIAL OCCASIONS

Galley Press

© 1985 Orbis Verlag
English language edition designed and produced by
Autumn Publishing Limited, 10 Eastgate Square,
Chichester, England.

Translation by Meckie Hellary
Editorial by Sherian Morgan
         Rosemary Blott

Published in this edition by Galley Press, an imprint
of W H Smith & Son Limited
Registered No 237811 England.
Trading as WHS Distributors, St John's House,
East Street, Leicester, LE1 6NE

Typeset by Avonset, Midsomer Norton, Bath, England.

Printed in Italy by GEA, Milan,
in association with Keats European Ltd.

ISBN 0–86136–695–6

Exact conversion to metric from imperial (28.35) does not
always give convenient working quantities. Therefore
metric quantities have been given in units of the nearest
25 grams, except where a different amount is necessary
to produce a balanced recipe.
Do be careful to follow 1 type of measure throughout the
recipe.
All recipes are for four people unless otherwise stated.

COOKERY INTERNATIONAL

SPECIAL OCCASIONS

CONTENTS

ANTIPASTI

These delicious hors d'oeuvres or antipasti are of Italian origin and present a marvellous opportunity to prepare all kinds of imaginative delicacies. Exact quantities cannot be given: it is best to assemble a platter with whatever is available in the refrigerator or larder. Here are some suggestions:

Chilled slices of melon wrapped in thin slices of smoked ham. Accompany with sliced celery and carrots, which have been marinated in a dressing of oil, vinegar, salt, and pepper.

Slices of smoked salmon, garnished with a slice of lemon topped with a little caviare. Add a few stuffed green olives.

Fill drained artichoke bases with Béarnaise Sauce. Garnish with black olives and radicchio.

Roll up some slices of Mortadella sausage and fill them with capers. Accompany with slices hardboiled egg and anchovy fillets.

Mix tinned tuna fish with marinaded artichoke hearts and garnish with strips of red pepper and celery leaves.

Marinade asparagus tips in oil, vinegar, salt, and pepper and garnish with a band of chopped hardboiled egg.

Season tomato wedges with salt and pepper, cover with slices of onion, and garnish with cocktail onions. Sprinkle lightly with oil and vinegar.

Serve with French bread or small crusty rolls and butter.

Use your imagination when preparing antipasti. Here are some ideas with which to start.

LOBSTER SCALLOPS

Preparation time: 25 mins.
About 390 calories/1632 joules

Metric/Imperial	American
½ round lettuce	½ round lettuce
250g/8 oz frozen lobster meat	½ lb frozen lobster meat
150g/5 oz mayonnaise	⅔ cup mayonnaise
2x15ml/2 tbs condensed milk or single cream	2 tbs condensed milk or light cream
juice ½ lemon	juice ½ lemon
salt, white pepper	salt, white pepper
pinch of sugar	pinch of sugar
1x15ml/1 tbs capers	1 tbs capers
1 hardboiled egg for garnish	1 hardboiled egg for garnish

Shred the lettuce finely and arrange it on 4 scallop shells. Flake the lobster meat and place it on the lettuce.

Mix the mayonnaise with the condensed milk or cream and lemon juice, and season with salt, pepper, and sugar. Pour over the lobster meat. Sprinkle with the capers, and garnish with slices of egg. Serve chilled.

Serve as a starter, a small snack for a special occasion, a light supper, or as part of a cold buffet.

MATJES WITH ALMONDS

Preparation time without soaking: 30 mins.
About 670 calories/2804 joules

Metric/Imperial	American
8 matjes fillets	8 matjes fillets
500ml/16 fl oz milk	2 cups milk
2 cooking apples	2 cooking apples
250/8 fl oz white wine	1 cup white wine
For the filling:	
½ eating apple	½ eating apple
1x5ml/1 tsp lemon juice	1 tsp lemon juice
100g/4 oz ground almonds	1 cup ground almonds
100g/4 oz quark or curd cheese	¼ lb quark or curd cheese
1x15ml/1 tbs grated horseradish	1 tbs grated horseradish
For the garnish:	
2x15ml/2 tbs cranberry sauce	2 tbs cranberry sauce

Matjes — is a herring which is not yet mature. It is at a stage when it is most tender and succullent. However, it also perishes easily, and so it is salted straight away.

Soak the matjes fillets in the milk for 2 or 3 hrs. Drain and dry them on kitchen paper.

Peel and core the apples and cut each apple in 4 slices. Bring the white wine to the boil and gently poach the apple slices for 5 mins. Remove the apples with a draining spoon and arrange them on a serving plate.

For the filling, finely grate ½ an apple and sprinkle it with lemon juice. Mix it with ⅔ of the ground almonds, the quark and the horseradish. Spread this mixture over the matjes fillets and roll them up. Carefully roll the stuffed matjes in the remaining ground almonds. Place the rolls upright on the apple slices and garnish the tops with small dots of cranberry sauce.

Serve as a starter or as part of a cold buffet.

BANANA COCKTAIL

Preparation time: 20 mins.
About 142 calories/594 joules

Metric/Imperial	American
3 bananas	3 bananas
3x15ml/3 tbs frozen peas	3 tbs frozen peas
100g/4 oz prawns	¼ lb shrimps
Sauce:	
2x15ml/2 tbs mayonnaise	2 tbs mayonnaise
3x15ml/3 tbs condensed milk or single cream	3 tbs condensed milk or light cream
1x15ml/1 tbs mango chutney	1 tbs mango chutney
1x15ml/1 tbs brandy	1 tbs brandy
salt, pepper	salt, pepper
a little sugar	a little sugar
4 lettuce leaves	4 lettuce leaves

This cocktail makes a very suitable starter to a special meal.
Slice the bananas, and cook the peas in boiling water for 8 mins. Cool them and then mix them with the bananas and prawns. Mix the mayonnaise with the condensed milk or cream, add the mango chutney and brandy and season with salt, pepper and sugar. Stir the sauce into the banana mixture. Line 4 sundae glasses with the lettuce leaves and arrange the cocktail on top.
Serve with toast and butter.

Caviare bouchées.

CAVIARE BOUCHÉES

Preparation time: 40 mins.
250 calories/1046 joules

Metric/Imperial	American
250g/8 oz frozen puff pastry	½ lb frozen puff paste
1 egg yolk	1 egg yolk
100g/4 oz caviare	¼ lb caviare
1 lemon	1 lemon

Preheat oven to 220°C/425°F/Gas 7.
Defrost the puff pastry according to instructions on the packet. Cut out 16 rounds, 4 cm/2'' in diameter. Cut the centres out of 8 rounds to make rings. Dampen the pastry pieces with cold water and place the rings on top of the bases. Brush the bouchées with beaten egg yolk and place them on a dampened baking sheet. Bake in the preheated oven on the centre shelf for 25 mins.
After cooling, fill the bouchées with the well chilled caviare and garnish with lemon wedges.

ANCHOVY EGGS

Preparation time: 30 mins.
About 275 calories/1151 joules

Metric/Imperial	American
8 hardboiled eggs	8 hardboiled eggs
2x15ml/2 tbs anchovy paste	2 tbs anchovy paste
a little lemon juice	a little lemon juice
2x15ml/2 tbs butter	2 tbs butter
2x15ml/2 tbs mayonnaise	2 tbs mayonnaise
pepper	pepper
For the garnish:	
1 tin of anchovy fillets	1 can of anchovy fillets
strips of pimento	strips of pimento
capers	capers
stuffed green olives	stuffed green olives
1 truffle	1 truffle
pistachio nuts, chopped	pistachio nuts, chopped
parsley, dill	parsley, dill

Halve the eggs and cut a sliver off the bottom of each half so that they stand level on the plate. Remove the yolks and beat them with the anchovy paste, lemon juice, butter, mayonnaise, and pepper until light and fluffy. Spoon the mixture into a piping bag fitted with a star nozzle and pipe it into the egg whites. Garnish with strips of anchovy fillets and pimento, capers, sliced olives, pieces of truffle, pistachio nuts, and sprigs of parsley and dill.

Banana cocktail.

ANCHOVY MOUSSE

Preparation time without chilling: 25 mins.
About 369 calories/1544 joules

Metric/Imperial	American
1 large tin of anchovy fillets	1 large can of anchovy fillets
1 onion	1 onion
2 hardboiled eggs	2 hardboiled eggs
100g/4 oz butter	½ cup butter
3 olives	3 olives
sprigs of dill	sprigs of dill

Drain and chop the anchovy fillets (reserving a few for garnish), onion, and eggs finely. Mix with a little of the anchovy liquor. Beat the butter until light and fluffy and stir it into the anchovy mixture. Firmly press the mixture into a round, greased dish and chill for 3 hrs. Invert the mousse on to a serving plate and garnish with olives, anchovy twists, and dill.

Serve with crusty brown bread and a mixed salad.

CHAMPAGNE BREAKFAST

Metric/Imperial	American
125ml/4 fl oz madeira	½ cup madeira
1x5ml/1 tsp gelatine	1 tsp gelatine
water for soaking	water for soaking
For the horseradish cream:	
125ml/4 fl oz whipping cream	½ cup whipping cream
pinch of caster sugar	pinch of granulated sugar
pinch of salt	pinch of salt
1x15ml/1 tbs horse-radish, grated	1 tbs horseradish, grated
For the mayonnaise:	
50g/2 oz mayonnaise	¼ cup mayonnaise
2x15ml/2 tbs soured cream	2 tbs sour cream
pinch of caster sugar	pinch of granulated sugar
For the scrambled eggs:	
3 eggs	3 eggs
salt, white pepper	salt, white pepper
3x15ml/3 tbs milk	3 tbs milk
25g/1 oz butter	2 tbs butter
few sprigs chives	few sprigs chives
In addition:	
100g/4 oz caviare or lumpfish roe	¼ lb caviare or lumpfish roe
100g/4 oz smoked salmon	¼ lb smoked salmon
100g/4 oz smoked sturgeon	¼ lb smoked sturgeon
250g/8 oz smoked eel	½ lb smoked eel
12 asparagus tips (tinned)	12 asparagus tips (canned)
4 slices cooked ham	4 slices cooked ham
2 hardboiled eggs	2 hardboiled eggs
2 lemons	2 lemons
100g/4 oz pressed tongue	¼ lb pressed tongue
few sprigs parsley	few sprigs parsley
French bread	French bread
toast, butter	toast, butter
2 bottles well chilled champagne	2 bottles well chilled champagne

A champagne breakfast is a good way of celebrating very special occasions. Its success does not only depend on what is served, but also how it is presented. It looks most attractive when arranged on a large silver serving dish lined with some lettuce leaves.

Gently heat the madeira in a saucepan. Soak the gelatine in a little cold water and dissolve it in the warm madeira. Rinse a deep plate with cold water and pour in the madeira jelly. Chill it in the refrigerator for about 2 hours until it is set. Invert the jelly on to a plate and chop it into small cubes.

For the horseradish cream, whip the cream until stiff and fold in the sugar, salt, and horseradish. Place it in the icemaking compartment of the refrigerator.

For the mayonnaise, stir the soured cream and sugar into the mayonnaise and chill.

In a bowl, beat the eggs with salt, pepper, and milk. Melt the butter in a frying pan and pour in the eggs. Leave until the bottom has set, then loosen the mixture from the sides so that the still liquid part cooks as well. Break up lightly with a fork and remove from the heat. Finely snip the chives.

Spoon the caviare into a small bowl. Roll up the sliced smoked salmon and sturgeon. Cut the smoked eel in 4 cm/2 in. pieces. Halve and skin them and remove the bones. Drain the asparagus tips. Place 3 tips on each slice of ham and spread the mayonnaise on top. Roll up the ham slices. Cut the hardboiled eggs in quarters and the lemons into 8 wedges. Slice the tongue. In the centre of a large serving plate, place a glass dish filled with ice cubes and set the bowl of caviare on top. Arrange the egg and lemon wedges around the caviare in a star pattern. Surround the centre with the remaining ingredients in the following way: the smoked salmon rolls with stars of horseradish cream piped on top, and the sturgeon rolls on either side. Lay the slices of tongue like fans at each end of the plate and top with the madeira jelly cubes. Next to the tongue, place the ham rolls, with the pieces of smoked eel in front. Distribute small portions of scrambled egg between the eel pieces, and sprinkle the snipped chives on top. Garnish with sprigs of parsley and serve with French bread, toast, and butter. And, of course, the well chilled champagne.

Ingredients of your choice could be substituted for any of these suggestions of what to serve at a champagne breakfast.

COLD PLATTER

Cold platters usually consist of an attractive arrangement of various sliced cold meats, sausages, and fish. Here are 4 suggestions:

1. Roll cooked and smoked slices of ham into cones and fill them with asparagus tips and mayonnaise. Cut some gherkins into fan shapes. Arrange the ham cones in the centre of a large serving plate lined with some fresh lettuce leaves. Garnish with the gherkins, and with slices or wedges of hardboiled egg, capers, and anchovy fillets. Surround with a selection of cold sliced meats (salami, liver sausage, etc.), garnished with cubed pineapple or mandarin oranges and tomatoes.

2. Completely cover a large serving plate with a selection of cold roast meats like beef, pork, or lamb, spiced silverside of beef, smoked pork loin, etc. Garnish with sliced cucumber or gherkins, parsley, and a small bowl of relish.

3. Prepare a cold platter with a selection of different kinds of preserved fish: smoked salmon, smoked trout, tuna fish, sardines in oil, marinated herrings etc. Try covering a wooden board with green lettuce leaves or with aluminium foil for serving. Accompany the salmon with a small dish of horseradish cream, add egg or olive slices for the tuna fish, and gherkins or pickled onions for the other fish.

4. This suggestion needs a complete recipe:

Metric/Imperial	American
For the marinade:	
2x15ml/2 tbs vinegar	2 tbs vinegar
4x15ml/4 tbs oil	4 tbs oil
1x15ml/1tbs warm water	1 tbs warm water
salt, sugar	salt, sugar
2½ml/½ tsp mustard	½ tsp mustard
In addition:	
½ a lettuce	½ a lettuce
12 tinned asparagus spears	12 canned asparagus spears
4 slices cooked ham	4 slices cooked ham
few sprigs chives	few sprigs chives
4 tomatoes	4 tomatoes
100g/4 oz cream cheese with herbs	¼ lb cream cheese with herbs
few sprigs parsley	few sprigs parsley
4 hardboiled eggs	4 hardboiled eggs
3x15ml/3 tbs tomato ketchup	3 tbs tomato ketchup
salt	salt
4 slices salami	4 slices salami
4x5ml/4 tsp horse-radish sauce	4 tsp horseradish sauce
4 slices liver pâté	4 slices liver pâté
4 slices Zungenwurst (German sausage)	4 slices Zungenwurst (German sausage)
few sprigs dill	few sprigs dill
1 gherkin	1 gherkin

COLD BEEF OLIVES

Preparation time: 45 mins.
About 380 calories/1590 joules

Metric/Imperial	American
1x15ml/1 tbs gelatine	1 tbs gelatine
100g/4 oz celeriac, grated	¼ lb celeriac, grated
juice ½ lemon	juice ½ lemon
1 eating apple	1 eating apple
1 tin of mandarin oranges	1 can of mandarin oranges
100g/4 oz mayonnaise	½ cup mayonnaise
2x15ml/2 tbs cranberry sauce	2 tbs cranberry sauce
salt, white pepper, caster sugar	salt, white pepper, granulated sugar
12 thin slices cold roast beef	12 thin slices cold roast beef
3 sprigs parsley	3 sprigs parsley
4 lemon wedges	4 lemon wedges

Soak the gelatine in a little cold water. Place the celeriac in a bowl and sprinkle it with half of the lemon juice. Peel and core the apple and grate it finely. Add it to the celeriac and sprinkle with the remaining lemon juice. Drain the mandarin oranges, reserving the syrup. Heat 6x15ml/6 tbs of mandarin syrup and dissolve the gelatine in it. Leave this to cool before stirring it into the mayonnaise with the cranberry sauce. Fold the celeriac, apple, and mandarin oranges into the mayonnaise and season with salt, pepper, and sugar. Spread the mixture over the slices of beef and roll them up. Leave to set in the refrigerator. Garnish with parsley sprigs and lemon wedges and serve.
Serve as part of a cold buffet, as a light lunch or supper dish, or as a starter for 6 people.

NOTE
You could replace the beef with thin slices of cold roast pork.

For the marinade, mix the vinegar, oil, and water and season with salt, sugar, and mustard. Separate the lettuce into bite-size pieces and roll them in the marinade. Remove the lettuce from the dressing, drain it, and arrange it on a large serving plate. Place the asparagus in the marinade for 5 mins. Place 3 asparagus spears on each slice of ham, roll them up, and arrange them on the plate. Finely snip the chives and sprinkle half of them over the ham rolls.

Cut off the tops of the tomatoes and remove the tomato flesh with a teaspoon. Beat the cream cheese until fluffy and spoon it into the tomato shells. Top with the lids and garnish with parsley. Place the stuffed tomatoes in the centre of the plate, halve the eggs lengthwise and remove the yolks. Mix the yolks with the tomato ketchup and season lightly with salt. Add the remaining chives and spoon the mixture back into the egg halves. Arrange the eggs on each side of the tomatoes. Roll the slices of salami into cones and fill each with 1x5ml/1 tsp of horseradish sauce. Place them on the serving plate, together with the slices of liver pâté and Zungenwurst. Garnish the pâté with chopped dill, and the Zungenwurst with slivers of gherkin. Serve with bread and butter.

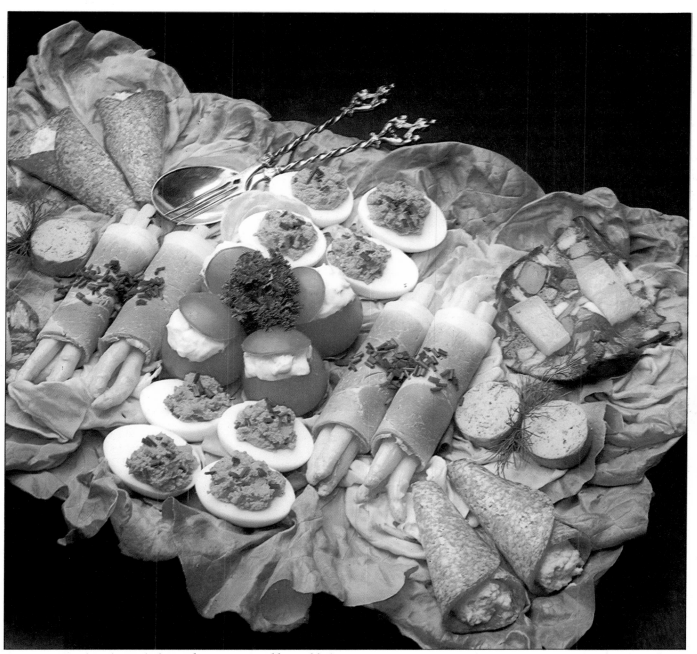

There is no end to the variations when you assemble a cold platter.

MEAT HORNS

The best way to prepare these meat horns is to buy the meat ready cooked: roast beef, pork, ham, and tongue. Allow about 100g/4 oz/¼ lb meat per person. The slices of meat are then filled as follows:

Beef with horseradish cream: whip 125ml/4 fl oz/ ½ cup whipping cream until stiff and fold in 4x5ml/4 tsp of grated horseradish. Season with salt, sugar, and pepper. Place on slices of beef, roll them up, and fasten them with cocktail sticks.

Pork with gherkins and mayonnaise: place gherkins and mayonnaise on the slices of pork, roll them up, and fasten them with cocktail sticks.

Ham with asparagus: place 3 asparagus spears on each slice of ham, cover them with mayonnaise, roll the slices up, and fasten.

Tongue with a salad of your choice: fill the slices of tongue and roll them up into a horn.

Arrange everything on a large serving plate and garnish with parsley and tomato and egg wedges, and serve with bread and butter.

The meat horns are filled with tasty surprises.

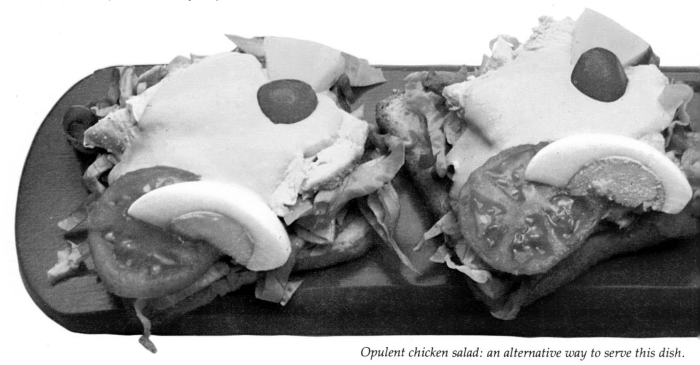

Opulent chicken salad: an alternative way to serve this dish.

OPULENT CHICKEN SALAD

Preparation time: 1¼ hrs.
About 340 calories/1423 joules

Metric/Imperial	American
250ml/8 fl oz water, salt	1 cup water, salt
2 chicken breasts, boned	2 chicken breasts, boned
For the dressing:	
4x15ml/4 tbs mayonnaise	4 tbs mayonnaise
2x15ml/2 tbs single cream	2 tbs light cream
1x5ml/1 tsp horseradish	1 tsp horseradish
1x15ml/1 tbs tomato ketchup	1 tbs tomato ketchup
juice ½ orange	juice ½ orange
2x15ml/2 tbs brandy	2 tbs brandy
salt, white pepper	salt, white pepper
For the garnish:	
1 lettuce	1 lettuce
4 hardboiled eggs	4 hardboiled eggs
4 tomatoes	4 tomatoes
2 slices tinned pineapple	2 slices canned pineapple

Bring the salted water to the boil and gently poach the chicken breasts for about 40 mins.

For the dressing, mix the mayonnaise, cream, horseradish, tomato ketchup, orange juice, and brandy together in a bowl, and season with salt and pepper. Chill Well.

Skin the chicken breasts and cut them into fine strips. Leave them to cool. Shred the lettuce finely and divide it between 4 glass dishes. Arrange the chicken on top and pour the dressing over. Cut the eggs into quarters and skin and slice the tomatoes. Drain the pineapple, and cut it into cubes. Garnish the chicken with the eggs, tomatoes and pineapple.

DANISH SMØRREBRØD

The various toppings for smørrebrød consist of fish, meat, cheese, or eggs with different garnishes. Smørrebrød can have a base of white or brown bread, rye, pumpernickel bread, or crispbread. Here are some suggestions for the toppings:

Cover the bread generously with sliced luncheon meat. Place a spoonful of grated horseradish in the centre and garnish with a twisted slice of orange, two prunes, and a little parsley.

Place a lettuce leaf on the bread and cover with a grilled chicken drumstick wrapped in a slice of bacon. Garnish with slices of cucumber and tomato and chopped cress.

Cover the bread with seasoned steak tartare and place a raw egg yolk in the centre. Surround the egg yolk with chopped raw onion and capers.

Place a lettuce leaf on the bread and cover with 3 thin slices of cold roast beef which have been rolled up and stuffed with glacé fruit. Garnish with gherkin fans.

Cover the bread first with lettuce and then with slices of hardboiled egg and tomatoes. Pipe a wide strip of mayonnaise across the centre and garnish with caviare or lumpfish roe.

Cut a slice of cheese to fit the bread and garnish with tomato wedges and cress.

Place 3 rolls of ham on the bread and spoon some vegetable salad on top in the centre. Garnish with egg, tomato, and cucumber slices and tiny sprigs of parsley.

Cover the bread with thin slices of smoked salmon and top with a little cold scrambled egg. Sprinkle with snipped chives.

Place a thick slice of liver pâté on the bread and top with thinly sliced cucumber and mushrooms.

Cover the bread thickly with salami and garnish with raw onion rings.

Place a lettuce leaf on the bread. Slice a hardboiled egg lengthwise and lay it in a row over the lettuce. Lay 2 slices of cured bacon alongside. Garnish with tomato wedges and cress.

Cover the bread with a thick slice of danish blue cheese. Place a raw egg yolk on top and garnish with an onion ring and sliced radishes.

Danish Smørrebrød: the bes

en sandwiches in Europe.

Smoked ham platter.

SMOKED HAM PLATTER

Preparation time: 45 mins.
About 230 calories/963 joules

Metric/Imperial

16 thin slices of very lean smoked ham, e.g. parma ham
75g/3 oz low fat soft cheese
1 small onion
few sprigs chives
salt, white pepper
1x5ml/1 tsp paprika pepper
125ml/4 fl oz whipping cream
2x15ml/2 tbs grated horseradish
1 pinch of sugar
For the garnish:
150g/5 oz sauerkraut
1 small apple
1 slice of pineapple
1x5ml/1 tsp lemon juice
salt
4 large tomatoes
3 pickled gherkins
2x15ml/2 tbs silver-skin onions
6 stuffed olives
few sprigs parsley

American

16 thin slices of very lean smoked ham, e.g. parma ham
¾ cup low fat soft cheese
1 small onion
few sprigs chives
salt, white pepper
1 tsp paprika pepper

½ cup whipping cream

2 tbs grated horse-radish
1 pinch of sugar

1 cup sauerkraut
1 small apple
1 slice of pineapple
1 tsp lemon juice

salt
4 large tomatoes
3 pickled gherkins
2 tbs cocktail onions
6 stuffed olives
few sprigs parsley

A smoked ham platter forms the ideal starter for a celebration dinner. But it could also be part of a cold buffet table.

Spread out 8 slices of ham on the work surface. Finely grate the onion and chop the chives. Mix with the low fat soft cheese and season well with salt, pepper and paprika pepper. Divide between 4 ham slices and roll up.

Whip the cream and stir in the horseradish, sugar and salt. Spread 4 ham slices with the mixture and roll up.

Cover a large serving platter with the remaining ham, overlapping the slices attractively. Place the stuffed ham rolls around the edge, leaving a space between every two rolls.

For the garnish, drain the sauerkraut and flake lightly with a fork. Finely chop the peeled apple and dice the pineapple. Stir into the sauerkraut. Season with lemon juice and salt and leave for a short time for the flavours to be absorbed.

Cut a lid off the tomatoes and with a teaspoon carefully remove the flesh. Fill the tomato shells with the sauerkraut mixture, replace the lid and place a tomato between every two ham rolls. Finely slice the gherkins, drain the onions and halve the olives. Use to garnish the platter. Arrange the parsley in small sprigs around the edge.

CHICKEN AND PEACH OPEN SANDWICHES

Preparation time: 25 mins.
About 420 calories/1758 joules

Metric/Imperial	American
4 slices white bread	4 slices white bread
40g/1½ oz butter	3 tbs butter
2 tinned peach halves	2 canned peach halves
100g/4 oz cream cheese	¼ lb cream cheese
3x15ml/3 tbs peach syrup	3 tbs peach syrup
salt, sugar, curry powder	salt, sugar, curry powder
1x5ml/1 tsp lemon juice	1 tsp lemon juice
300g/10 oz cooked chicken, diced	10 oz cooked chicken, diced
For the garnish:	
4 lettuce leaves	4 lettuce leaves
2 tinned peach halves	2 canned peach halves
4 cocktail cherries	4 cocktail cherries
4 twists of lemon	4 twists of lemon
4 sprigs parsley	4 sprigs parsley

Spread the slices of bread with butter. Purée the peach halves and mix with the cream cheese and peach syrup. Season well with salt, sugar, curry powder, and lemon juice. Fold in the diced chicken and divide the mixture between the slices of bread. Place a lettuce leaf on each of 4 plates and put an open sandwich on top. Garnish each with 2 slices of peach, a cocktail cherry, a twist of lemon, and a sprig of parsley.

GOURMET ROLLS

Preparation time: 45 mins.
About 425 calories/1779 joules

Metric/Imperial	American
300g/10 oz prawns (fresh or frozen)	10 oz shrimps (fresh or frozen)
4 bread rolls	4 bread rolls
60g/2½ oz butter	⅓ cup butter
2 small onions	2 small onions
300g/10 oz button mushrooms	10 oz mushrooms
6x15ml/6 tbs dry white wine	6 tbs dry white wine
3x15ml/3 tbs milk	3 tbs milk
6x15ml/6 tbs single cream	6 tbs light cream
1 egg yolk	1 egg yolk
salt, white pepper	salt, white pepper
few sprigs parsley	few sprigs parsley

Preheat oven to 250°C/475°F/Gas 9.
Defrost and drain the prawns if frozen. Cut off the tops of the rolls and scoop out the centres. Melt 2x15ml/2 tbs of the butter and brush the rolls inside and out. Place them in the preheated oven on the centre shelf for 5 mins.
Finely chop the onions and fry them in the remaining butter until transparent. Slice the mushrooms and add them to the onions. Fry for 10 mins. Stir in the white wine and milk, and bring to the boil. Remove from the heat and stir in the cream and egg yolk. Season with salt and pepper. Fold in the prepared prawns and heat through. Spoon the mixture into the hot rolls and garnish with parsley. Serve immediately.
Serve Gourmet Rolls as a light lunch or supper dish.

Gourmet rolls as a light lunch or supper dish.

LEEK AND HAM QUICHE

Serves 6.

Preparation time: 1 hr. 25 mins.
About 775 calories/3244 joules

Metric/Imperial	American
For the filling:	
500g/1 lb leeks	1 lb leeks
250ml/8 fl oz water, salt	1 cup water, salt
100g/4 oz streaky bacon, diced	6 fatty bacon slices, diced
150g/5 oz cooked ham, diced	5 oz cooked ham, diced
3 eggs	3 eggs
125ml/4 fl oz soured cream	½ cup sour cream
4x15ml/4 tbs single cream	4 tbs light cream
white pepper, grated nutmeg	white pepper, grated nutmeg
For the pastry:	
125g/4 oz plain flour	1 cup all purpose flour
2½ml/½ tsp baking powder	½ tsp double acting baking powder
pinch of salt	pinch of salt
40g/1½ oz butter or margarine	3 tbs butter or margarine
2½ml/½ tsp mustard powder	½ tsp mustard powder
pinch each of dried tarragon, lemon balm and mint	pinch each of dried tarragon, lemon balm and mint
100g/4 oz Cheddar cheese, grated	¼ lb Cheddar cheese, grated
1 onion	1 onion
1 egg	1 egg
2x15ml/2 tbs milk	2 tbs milk
margarine for greasing	margarine for greasing

Preheat oven to 200°C/400°F/Gas 6.

For the filling, thickly slice the leeks and cook them in boiling salted water for 5 mins. Drain and cool them. Fry the diced bacon until the fat runs. Drain and cool it, and mix with the leeks and diced ham. Beat the eggs with the soured cream, cream, salt, pepper, and nutmeg and set aside.

For the pastry, sift the four, baking powder, and salt into a bowl. Dice the butter or margaine and rub into the flour. Add the mustard powder, herbs, grated cheese and finely chopped onion. Make a hollow in the centre and stir in the beaten egg and milk. Mix together with a knife, and then knead to a smooth dough with your hands.

Grease a 26cm/10 in. flan tin with removable base,

and line it with the pastry. Spread the leek, bacon, and ham mixture over the base and pour the eggs and cream over. Bake in the preheated oven on the bottom shelf for 45 mins.

Serve warm.

Serve as a lunch or supper dish with a green salad.

HANGOVER BREAKFAST

Preparation time without soaking: 30 mins.
About 290 calories/1214 joules

Metric/Imperial	American
8 matjes fillets	8 matjes fillets
250ml/8 fl oz water	1 cup water
6x15ml/6 tbs milk	6 tbs milk
For the marinade:	
125ml/4 fl oz soured cream	½ cup sour cream
salt, black pepper	salt, black pepper
pinch of sugar	pinch of sugar
In addition:	
½ a lettuce	½ a lettuce
1 large tart apple	1 large tart apple
2 small onions	2 small onions
1 gherkin	1 gherkin
1x15ml/1 tbs capers	1 tbs capers

Soak the matjes fillets overnight in a mixture of water and milk. Whip the chilled soured cream and season with salt, plenty of pepper, and sugar. Return to the refrigerator. Line 4 individual glass dishes with lettuce. Drain the matjes fillets and pat dry on kitchen paper. Cut them into bite-sized pieces. Peel, core, quarter, and slice the apple. Thinly slice the onions, and dice the gherkin. Fill the glass dishes with alternate layers of fish, apple, onion, and gherkin. Roughly chop the capers and sprinkle them over the dishes. Pour over the marinade and serve immediately.

Serve with buttered wholemeal bread, and cool beer or mineral water.

Hangover breakfast.

A tasty addition to a barbecue: oriental fish kebabs.

ORIENTAL FISH KEBABS

Preparation time: 45 mins.
About 495 calories/2072 joules

Metric/Imperial

1kg/2¼ lbs fillet of
  of cod or haddock
For the marinade:
juice 2 lemons
1 clove garlic,
  salt
In addition:
8 small tomatoes
4 small onions
4x15ml/4 tbs olive
  oil
2x15ml/2 tbs sherry
1x5ml/1 tsp sugar
salt, white pepper
For the sauce:
150ml/5 oz natural
  yogurt
125ml/4 fl oz soured
  cream
few sprigs parsley
few sprigs chives
salt

American

2¼ lbs fillet of cod
  or haddock

juice 2 lemons
1 clove garlic,
  salt

8 small tomatoes
4 small onions
4 tbs olive oil

2 tbs sherry
1 tsp sugar
salt, white pepper

⅔ cup natural yogurt

½ cup sour cream

few sprigs parsley
few sprigs chives
salt

Oriental fish kebabs taste equally good barbecued or grilled. Rinse the fillets of fish under cold water and pat dry. Cut across into finger-thick slices. Mix the lemon juice with the crushed garlic and salt and place the fish in the mixture for about 15 mins.

Meanwhile, quarter the tomatoes. Peel and quarter the onions and blanch them briefly in boiling water. Drain the fish strips and roll them up. Thread the fish rolls, tomato and onion quarters on to 4 skewers. Place the kebabs on a grill rack. Mix 2x15ml/2 tbs of the marinade with the oil, sherry, sugar, salt, and plenty of pepper and brush this over the kebabs. Grill or barbecue the kebabs for 10 mins., turning and brushing them frequently with the sherry marinade.

For the sauce, whip the yogurt with the soured cream and stir in the finely chopped parsley and chives. Season with salt. Serve with the cooked fish kebabs.

Serve with a green salad and boiled rice or jacket potatoes.

MUSHROOM KEBABS

Preparation time: 40 mins.
Altogether about 365 calories/1527 joules

Metric/Imperial	American
2x15ml/2 tbs oil	2 tbs oil
salt, white pepper	salt, white pepper
500g/1 lb mushrooms	1 lb mushrooms
4 small tomatoes	4 small tomatoes
lemon juice	lemon juice
few sprigs parsley	few sprigs parsley

Season the oil with salt and pepper. Wipe and trim the mushrooms and marinade them in the oil for 5 mins. Drain and thread the mushrooms on to 4 skewers. Make a cross cut in the tops of the tomatoes, remove the stalk ends, and thread one on to each mushroom skewer. Brush all over with the marinade and grill for 5 mins. Before serving, sprinkle with lemon juice and garnish with parsley. Serve with Béarnaise sauce.

CURRIED KEBABS

Preparation time: 20 mins.
About 270 calories/1130 joules

Metric/Imperial	American
2 slices tinned pineapple	2 slices canned pineapple
250g/8 oz fillet of pork	½ lb fillet of pork
4 slices streaky bacon	4 fatty bacon slices
2 small onions	2 small onions
2 bananas	2 bananas
2x15ml/2 tbs oil	2 tbs oil
4x5ml/4 tsp curry powder	4 tsp curry powder

Drain the pineapple and cut it into 8 cubes. Dice the pork and bacon. Peel and slice the onions and bananas. Thread all the ingredients on to 4 skewers and fry in the hot oil for 10 mins. until golden. Sprinkle with curry powder and serve very hot. Serve with boiled rice or French bread.

Curried kebabs.

Tasty kebabs, kebabs with pineapple, Iranian kebabs.

TASTY KEBABS

Preparation time without marinading: 1 hr.
About 495 calories/2072 joules

Metric/Imperial	American
For the marinade:	
2 onions	2 onions
2x15ml/2 tbs red-currant jelly	2 tbs redcurrant jelly
10 peppercorns	10 peppercorns
1¼ml/¼ tsp ground ginger	¼ tsp ground ginger
In addition:	
750g/1½ lbs fillet of pork	1½ lbs fillet of pork
50g/2 oz butter	¼ cup butter
2x15ml/2 tbs water	2 tbs water
2x15ml/2 tbs peanut	2 tbs peanut-butter
2½ml/½ tsp ground cinnamon	½ tsp ground cinnamon
1¼ml/¼ tsp ground cloves	¼ tsp ground cloves
2x5ml/2 tsp cornflour	2 tsp cornstarch
3x15ml/3 tbs natural yogurt	3 tbs natural yogurt

For the marinade, grate the onions and mix them with the redcurrant jelly in a large bowl. Crush the peppercorns and stir them into the mixture with the ginger. Cut the pork fillet in 3cm/1 in. cubes and leave in the marinade for 2 hrs.

Drain the meat, scraping off any bits of the marinade, and thread it on to 4 skewers. Melt the butter and stir in the water and peanut butter. Season with cinnamon and cloves. Stir in the cornflour and yogurt, and brush this mixture all over the kebabs. Grill them for about 50 mins., brushing frequently with the peanut butter mixture. Serve hot.

KEBABS WITH PINEAPPLE

Preparation time without soaking: 45 mins.
About 415 calories/1737 joules

Metric/Imperial	American
8 prunes	8 prunes
60ml/2½ fl oz red wine	¼ cup red wine
2 slices of tinned pineapple	2 slices of canned pineapple
2x15ml/2 tbs white rum	2 tbs white rum
500g/1 lb fillet of pork	1 lb fillet of pork
8 cocktail sausages	8 cocktail sausages
3x15ml/3 tbs oil	3 tbs oil
1x5ml/1 tsp mild mustard	1 tsp mild mustard
1x5ml/1 tsp paprika	1 tsp paprika

Soak the prunes overnight in the red wine. Drain the pineapple slices and place them on a plate. Sprinkle with the rum and leave for 1 hr. Rinse the pork under cold water and pat dry. Cut it into 2cm/1 in. slices. Drain the prunes and pineapple. Cut the pineapple slices in quarters. Thread 4 skewers with alternate pieces of meat, sausages, prunes, and pineapple. Mix together the oil, mustard, and paprika and brush this over the kebabs. Grill them for about 20 mins. until golden, brushing frequently with the oil mixture.

IRANIAN KEBABS

Preparation time without marinading: 1 hr.
About 890 calories/3725 joules

Metric/Imperial	American
For the marinade:	
5 large onions	5 large onions
1 clove garlic	1 clove garlic
125ml/4 fl oz soured cream	½ cup sour cream
1 bay leaf	1 bay leaf
10 peppercorns	10 peppercorns
In addition:	
750g/1½ lb lean, boneless lamb	1½ lbs lean, boneless lamb
For the dressing:	
1 onion	1 onion
juice 2 lemons	juice 2 lemons
salt	salt
125ml/4 fl oz oil	½ cup oil
few sprigs parsley	few sprigs parsley

Finely mince the onions and garlic and mix with the soured cream. Crumble the bay leaf and crush the peppercorns and add them to the onion mixture. Cut the lamb into 3cm/1 in. cubes and place in the marinade. Cover and leave for 3 hrs.
Remove the meat from the marinade and thread it on to 4 skewers. Grill the kebabs for about 40 mins. until crisp and golden. Turn the skewers frequently during grilling.
Meanwhile, prepare the dressing. Finely grate the onion and mix it with the lemon juice and salt. Stir in the oil and beat until the mixture emulsifies. Garnish the kebabs with parsley and serve the dressing separately.

ROQUEFORT BOATS

Preparation time: 50 mins.
About 610 calories/2553 joules

Metric/Imperial	American
250g/8 oz frozen puff pastry	½ lb frozen puff paste
For the filling:	
50g/2 oz butter and 50g/2 oz quark cheese or	¼ cup butter and 2 oz quark cheese or
100g/4 oz cream cheese	¼ lb cream cheese
200g/6 oz Roquefort cheese	6 oz Roquefort cheese
2x15ml/2 tbs sweet sherry	2 tbs sweet sherry
pinch of sugar, salt	pinch of sugar, salt
2 sticks celery	2 sticks celery
For the garnish:	
1 tomato	1 tomato
2 sprigs parsley	2 sprigs parsley

Preheat oven to 220°C/425°F/Gas 7.

Defrost the puff pastry according to instructions on the packet. Roll it out evenly and cut into 8 pieces. Rinse 8 boat-shaped tins with cold water and line them with the pastry. Prick the pastry several times with a fork and bake blind in the preheated oven for 30 mins.

Invert the baked boat shapes on to a wire rack and leave to cool. Meanwhile, for the filling, either beat the butter and quark together until light and fluffy or beat the cream cheese until fluffy. Crumble the Roquefort with a fork and mix into the cheese mixture. Season with sweet sherry, sugar, and salt. Chop the celery and stir it into the Roquefort cream. Fill the cooled pastry boats with the mixture and garnish with tomato wedges and parsley.

Roquefort boats.

MEAT BALLS WITH ROQUEFORT

Preparation time: 45 mins.
About 570 calories/2386 joules

Metric/Imperial

500g/1 lb mixed
   minced meat
   (beef, pork)
1 clove of garlic
8x15ml/8 tbs dried
   breadcrumbs
1 small onion
1 egg
salt, black pepper
50g/2 oz Roquefort
   cheese
1x5ml/1 tsp water
1 egg
oil for deep frying

American

1 lb mixed ground
   meat (beef, pork)

1 clove of garlic
8 tbs dried bread-
   crumbs
1 small onion
1 egg
salt, black pepper
½ cup Roquefort
   cheese
1 tsp water
1 egg
oil for deep frying

Mix the minced meat with the crushed garlic, 4x15ml/4 tbs of the breadcrumbs, chopped onion, and egg, and season with salt and pepper. Shape the mixture into 12 thin rounds. Stir the Roquefort with the water until smooth. Spread this over the centre of 6 of the meat rounds and cover with the remaining rounds. Seal the edges firmly and shape the patties into balls. Roll them first in beaten egg and then in the remaining breadcrumbs and deep fry in hot oil for 10 mins.

TIP

You can prepare the meat balls with Roquefort in a different way by mixing the Roquefort cheese with the minced meat, or by cutting the cheese into cubes and placing one inside each meat ball.

CHEESE PUFFS

Makes 25.

Preparation time: 1 hr. 20 mins.
About 95 calories/398 joules

Metric/Imperial

For the choux pastry:
250ml/8 fl oz water
50g/2 oz butter
pinch of salt
100g/4 oz plain flour

4 eggs
50g/2 oz soft herb
   cheese
margarine for greasing

For the fillings:
250ml/8 fl oz whipping
   cream
salt, pepper
paprika
65g/2½ oz cream cheese
15g/½ oz hard herb
   cheese, grated
50g/2 oz Emmenthal
   cheese, grated
few sprigs parsley

American

1 cup water
¼ cup butter
pinch of salt
1 cup all purpose
   flour

4 eggs
¼ cup soft herb
   cheese
margarine for
   greasing

1 cup whipping
   cream
salt, pepper
paprika
⅓ cup cream cheese
1 tbs hard herb
   cheese, grated
½ cup Swiss cheese,
   grated
few sprigs parsley

Preheat oven to 220°C/425°F/Gas 7.

Bring the water, butter and salt to the boil in a shallow saucepan. Remove from the heat and quickly beat in the sifted flour all at once. Return the pan to the heat and continue stirring over a low heat until the mixture forms a smooth ball and leaves the sides of the pan clean. Remove the pan from the heat again and stir in the 1st egg. Then leave the dough to cool for 5 mins. Continue stirring in the eggs one after the other until the previous egg has been completely absorbed. The dough should be smooth and shiny and just stiff enough to fall from the spoon. Break up the soft herb cheese with a fork and stir it into the mixture.

Grease a baking sheet and sprinkle it lightly with flour. Spoon the mixture into a piping bag and pipe small mounds on to the baking sheet. Place in the preheated oven on the centre shelf and bake for 45 mins.

Do not open the oven door during the first 20 mins. After 25 mins. cover the pastry puffs with greaseproof paper.

Remove the baking sheet from the oven and cool the puffs before slitting them open.

For the fillings, whip the cream until stiff and season with salt, pepper, and paprika. Beat the cream cheese until fluffy, then fold in gently half of the whipped cream and the grated herb cheese. Cover and chill in the refrigerator.

Sprinkle the grated Emmenthal cheese over the remaining whipped cream. Finely chop the parsley and add to the cream. Fold in gently. Spoon each filling into a piping bag and pipe them on to the bottom halves of the cooked pastry puffs. Cover with the lids and serve immediately.

Asiatic delicacies: Indian prawn balls.

INDIAN PRAWN BALLS

Preparation time: 35 mins.
About 290 calories/1214 joules

Metric/Imperial	American
375g/12 oz frozen prawns	12 oz frozen shrimps
2 onions	2 onions
few sprigs parsley	few sprigs parsley
3 sprigs fresh or 2½ml/½ tbs dried mint	2 sprigs fresh or ½ tbs dried mint
1 slice white bread	1 slice white bread
salt, white pepper	salt, white pepper
2½ml/½ tsp ground ginger	½ tsp ground ginger
1 egg	1 egg
4x15ml/4 tbs lemon juice	4 tbs lemon juice
6x15ml/6 tbs pease- meal	6 tbs pease-meal
1x5ml/1 tsp ground coriander	1 tsp ground coriander
1 dash of Tabasco sauce	1 dash of Tabasco sauce
2x15ml/2 tbs cold water	2 tbs cold water
4x15ml/4 tbs oil	4 tbs oil
1 lemon for garnish	1 lemon for garnish

Defrost the prawns and finely chop the onions, parsley and fresh mint. Cut the crusts off the bread and dice it finely. Mix the prawns with the onions, parsley, mint, bread cubes, salt, pepper and ginger. Add the egg and lemon juice and beat well with a wooden spoon until the mixture is smooth. Leave at room temperature for 30 mins.

Mix the pease-meal, coriander, Tabasco sauce, water and a little salt to a thick, smooth paste. Form the prawn mixture into balls, about 2cm/1 in. in diameter. Heat the oil in a frying pan until very hot. Spread the pease-meal paste all over the prawn balls, and fry them in the oil for 5 mins. each side. Arrange the browned and crisp prawn balls on a preheated serving dish and garnish with wedges of lemon.

BRAZILIAN EMPANADAS

Preparation time: 40 mins.
945 calories/3956 joules

Metric/Imperial	American
500g/1 lb frozen puff pastry	1 lb frozen puff paste
1 large onion	1 large onion
1x15ml/1 tbs butter	1 tbs butter
50g/2 oz streaky bacon, diced	3 fatty bacon slices, diced
200g/6 oz minced beef	1½ cups ground beef
salt, pepper	salt, pepper
cayenne pepper, paprika	cayenne pepper, paprika
2 hardboiled eggs	2 hardboiled eggs
12 stuffed green olives	12 stuffed green olives
5x15ml/5 tbs raisins	5 tbs raisins

Preheat the oven to 220°C/425°F/Gas 7.
Defrost the puff pastry according to instructions on the packet. Dice the onion and fry in the melted butter with the bacon until transparent. Add the minced beef and cook well. Season with the salt and peppers. Pour 4x15ml/4 tbs of water over the meat to prevent it from becoming too dry. Roughly chop the eggs and olives and stir them into the meat with the raisins. Taste for seasoning. Roll out the pastry and cut it into 8 rectangles. Spoon some of the beef mixture on to each rectangle. Brush the edges with water and fold the pastry over to make pockets. Bake in the preheated oven for 20 mins.

Brazilian empanadas are filled with a savoury beef mixture.

CRUDITÉS PLATTER

Preparation time: 50 mins.
About 360 calories/1506 joules

Metric/Imperial	American
For the yogurt dressing:	
2x15ml/2 tbs natural yogurt	2 tbs natural yogurt
1x5ml/1 tsp mayonnaise	1 tsp mayonnaise
pinch of salt	pinch of salt
2x5ml/2 tsp lemon juice	2 tsp lemon juice
For the lemon dressing:	
3x15ml/3 tbs lemon juice	3 tbs lemon juice
5x15ml/5 tbs oil	5 tbs oil
salt, pinch of sugar	salt, pinch of sugar
For the oil and vinegar dressing:	
1¼ml/¼ tsp dried tarragon	¼ tsp dried tarragon
4x15ml/4 tbs herb vinegar	4 tbs herb vinegar
1 onion	1 onion
salt, freshly ground black pepper	salt, freshly ground black pepper
pinch of sugar	pinch of sugar
8x15ml/8 tbs oil	8 tbs oil
For the crudités:	
150g/6 oz carrots, grated	6 oz carrots, grated
few sprigs dill	few sprigs dill
4 large cauliflower florets	4 large cauliflower florets
1 bunch radishes	1 bunch radishes
¼ cucumber	¼ cucumber
2 tomatoes	2 tomatoes
50g/2 oz lambs' lettuce	2 oz lambs' lettuce
small round lettuce	small round lettuce
small punnet cress	small punnet cress
few sprigs chives	few sprigs chives

A crudités platter, full of valuable vitamins and minerals.

Only use really fresh and good quality ingredients. The fresher the salads, vegetables and fruit, the more vitamins they contain.

Wash lettuces, vegetables and fruit whole, so that they will retain as many of the valuable vitamins as possible.

Prepare crudités as near to the time they will be served as possible.

Larger vegetables should be chopped finely to make them easier to digest. If you have to keep the ingredients for a little while, make sure they are well covered.

To improve the natural flavours, use plenty of fresh herbs. You can use dried herbs, but they only really develop their flavour after they have been soaked in a marinade of lemon juice or vinegar for about 10 mins.

For the yogurt dressing, mix the yogurt with the mayonnaise and season with salt and lemon juice.

For the lemon dressing, beat the lemon juice, oil, salt and sugar together.

For the oil and vinegar dressing, soak the tarragon in the vinegar for 10 mins., add the chopped onion and season with salt, pepper and sugar. Stir in the oil and mix well.

Wash and trim the vegetables. Mix the grated carrots with half of the lemon dressing and 1x15ml/1 tsp chopped dill.

Separate the cauliflower into tiny florets and mix them with the yogurt dressing.

Finely slice the radishes, cucumber and tomatoes. Separate the lettuces into small pieces. Arrange all the ingredients attractively on a large serving plate, sprinkle with chopped dill, cress and chives and serve with the remaining dressings.

STUFFED EGGS

Stuffed eggs can be served on many occasions. They make pretty additions to a cold buffet, delicious canapés for a drinks party, or an elegant starter for a special dinner.

Before you start, hardboil the eggs and cool them under running cold water. Peel and halve them. Carefully remove the yolks and rub them through a sieve. Then prepare the fillings:

With prawns:
Mix the egg yolks with mayonnaise and season with salt and pepper. Pipe into the egg halves and garnish with prawns and dill.

With Roquefort:
Mix the egg yolks with Roquefort cheese, butter and Worcester sauce. Add finely chopped olives and crumbled fried bacon. Spoon into the egg halves and garnish with sliced olives and parsley.

Mortimer:
Cut the hardboiled eggs in half horizontally and slice a small piece off the bottom to make them stable. Carefully remove the egg yolks and fill the whites with caviare. Roll up some anchovy fillets and place them on top of the caviare. Top with a sliver of truffle. Glaze the eggs with aspic jelly. Chill any remaining aspic and cut it into cubes when set. Place each egg half on a marinaded artichoke base and garnish with the diced aspic jelly.

With tomato cream:
Mix the egg yolks with tomato purée and soured cream and season with salt. Pipe into the egg halves and garnish with asparagus tips and dill.

Christopher Columbus:
Mix the egg yolks with finely chopped cooked chicken, anchovy fillets, capers and cucumber and spoon this into the egg halves. Arrange them on lettuce leaves and garnish with mayonnaise mixed with a little mustard and sliced radishes.

Eggs in cheese batter.

EGGS IN CHEESE BATTER

Preparation time: 25 mins.
About 270 calories/1130 joules

Metric/Imperial	American
For the cheese batter:	
125ml/4 fl oz milk	½ cup milk
25g/1 oz butter	2 tbs butter
salt	salt
50g/2 oz plain flour	½ cup all purpose flour
1 egg	1 egg
50g/2 oz Emmenthal cheese, grated	½ cup Swiss cheese, grated
pinch of nutmeg	pinch of nutmeg
4 hardboiled eggs	4 hardboiled eggs
oil for deep frying	oil for deep frying
4 lettuce leaves	4 lettuce leaves
2x5ml/2 tsp mustard	2 tsp mustard

Bring the milk with the butter and salt to the boil. Pour in the sifted flour all at once and stir over a low heat until the mixture no longer sticks to the pan. Remove from the heat and stir in the egg, cheese, and nutmeg. With wet hands, roll the hardboiled eggs in the batter and deep fry them in the hot oil for 5–10 mins. until golden. Halve the cooked eggs and arrange them on the lettuce leaves. Garnish each with a spot of mustard and serve.

EGGS IN ASPIC

Preparation time: 1½ hrs.
About 210 calories/880 joules

Metric/Imperial

5 hardboiled eggs
175g/6 oz button
   mushrooms, cooked
2 pimentos in brine
200g/7 oz tinned
   asparagus tips
few sprigs parsley
For the aspic:
2x15ml/2 tbs gelatine
   or aspic powder
500ml/16 fl oz hot
   chicken stock
salt, pepper
pinch of sugar, dash
   of vinegar
For the garnish:
parsley
10 extra mushrooms

American

5 hardboiled eggs
6 oz mushrooms,
   cooked
2 pimentos in brine
7 oz canned
   asparagus tips
few sprigs parsley

2 tbs gelatine or
   aspic powder
2 cups hot chicken
   stock
salt, pepper
pinch of sugar, dash
   of vinegar

parsley
10 extra mushrooms

Slice the eggs thickly. Drain the pimentos and asparagus tips. Slice the mushrooms and cut the pimentos in strips.   Divide the parsley into sprigs. Soak the gelatine in a little cold water and dissolve it in the hot stock. Season with salt, pepper, sugar and vinegar. Cover the bottom of a wetted bowl with some aspic and leave it to set. Place on it a layer of egg slices, mushrooms, pimentos, asparagus and parsley, arranging them in an attractive pattern. Brush with some more aspic and leave to set. Repeat this process until all the ingredients and the aspic are used up. Chill in the refrigerator until completely set. Before serving, dip the bowl briefly in hot water and invert it on to a serving plate. Garnish with parsley and mushrooms.

Eggs in aspic.

Danish cucumber.

DANISH CUCUMBER

Preparation time: 25 mins.
About 180 calories/753 joules

Metric/Imperial	American
1 large cucumber	1 large cucumber
5x15ml/5 tbs vinegar	5 tbs vinegar
4x15ml/4 tbs oil	4 tbs oil
salt, pepper	salt, pepper
For the filling:	
75g/3 oz smoked salmon, chopped	3 oz smoked salmon, chopped
50g/2 oz marinaded herring fillets, chopped	2 oz marinaded herring fillets, chopped
1 hardboiled egg, chopped	1 hardboiled egg, chopped
2x5ml/2 tsp grated horseradish	2 tsp grated horseradish
salt, pepper	salt, pepper
For the garnish:	
few sprigs parsley	few sprigs parsley
1 tomato	1 tomato

Danish cucumber provides a refreshing summer lunch or supper and it could also be served as a starter.

Wash the cucumber and, if preferred, peel it thinly. Cut it into about 8 lengths of 4cm/1½ in. Scoop out most of the centre of each piece to make a hollow. Mix the vinegar with the oil and salt and pepper and marinade the cucumber pieces in this for 15 mins, turning occasionally.

Remove the cucumber from the marinade, drain, and pat dry. Place the pieces upright on a serving dish.

For the filling, place the smoked salmon, herring, and egg into a bowl and add the horseradish and remaining marinade. Mix well, season and spoon into the cucumber hollows. Garnish with small sprigs of parsley and tomato wedges.

MUSHROOMS À LA GRÊCQUE

Preparation time: 30 mins.
Altogether about 395 calories/1653 joules

Metric/Imperial	American
250g/8 oz mushrooms	½ lb mushrooms
1 glass of white wine	1 glass of white wine
1 glass of water	1 glass of water
3x15ml/3 tbs olive oil	3 tbs olive oil
juice ½ lemon	juice ½ lemon
small bay leaf	small bay leaf
1 clove garlic, chopped	1 clove garlic, chopped
4 peppercorns	4 peppercorns
1 sprig each dill, parsley, chervil, and lovage	1 sprig each dill, parsley, chervil, and lovage

Mushrooms à la grêcque are often served with other hors d'oevres and vegetables cooked in the Greek style, like artichoke hearts, asparagus tips, or celery.

Wipe and trim the mushrooms. Bring the wine, water, olive oil and lemon juice to the boil with the flavourings and herbs (you can substitute 1x5m/1 tsp dried herbs for each of the fresh ones). Add the mushrooms and simmer for 6–8 mins. over a low heat. Leave the mushrooms to cool in the liquor and serve them cold.

Serve with French bread or toast and butter.

Cheese stuffed peppers should always be served well chilled.

Cheese tomatoes.

CHEESE STUFFED PEPPERS

Preparation time without chilling: 25 mins.
About 595 calories/2490 joules

Metric/Imperial	American
1 green and 1 red pepper	1 green and 1 red pepper
175g/6 oz cream cheese	6 oz cream cheese
75g/3 oz Roquefort cheese	3 oz Roquefort cheese
2x15ml/2 tbs butter	2 tbs butter
salt, white pepper	salt, white pepper
In addition:	
6 slices pumpernickel bread	6 slices pumpernickel bread
6 slices white bread	6 slices white bread
50g/2 oz grapes, halved	2 oz grapes, halved
6 stuffed olives, halved	6 stuffed olives, halved

If you run out of ideas for party snacks you should try these savoury and refreshing stuffed peppers.
Cut off the stalk ends of the peppers and remove the seeds. In a bowl, mix the cream cheese with the Roquefort and butter and beat until creamy. Season with salt and pepper. Press the mixture into the peppers, making sure there are no air pockets. Wrap the peppers in aluminium foil and chill in the refrigerator for 2 hrs. Before serving, cut the peppers into 12 slices with a sharp knife. Halve and butter both kinds of bread slices and place a slice of stuffed pepper on each slice of bread. Decorate with halved grapes and olives.
NOTE
For a different stuffing, substitute the Roquefort cheese with chopped tomatoes, onions, capers and tinned mushrooms.

CHEESE TOMATOES

Preparation time: 20 mins.
About 210 calories/879 joules

Metric/Imperial	American
4 large, firm tomatoes	4 large, firm tomatoes
150g/5 oz blue cheese	1¼ cups blue cheese
2x15ml/2 tbs single cream	2 tbs light cream
50g/2 oz celery, chopped	2 oz celery, chopped
salt, paprika	salt, paprika
4 large lettuce leaves	4 large lettuce leaves
few sprigs chives	few sprigs chives

Cut a lid off the top of each tomato and set aside. Scoop out the centre of the tomatoes. Mix the blue cheese with the cream until smooth and add the celery and seasoning. Spoon the cheese mixture into the hollow tomatoes and place one on each lettuce leaf on a serving plate. Sprinkle with snipped chives, replace the lids and serve.
Serve as a light starter or as part of a cold buffet.

STUFFED PEARS

Preparation time: 20 mins.
About 195 calories/816 joules

Metric/Imperial	American
8 tinned pear halves	8 canned pear halves
juice 1 lemon	juice 1 lemon
For the filling:	
100g/4 oz quark or curd cheese	¼ lb quark or curd cheese
1x15ml/1 tbs mayonnaise	1 tbs mayonnaise
1x15ml/1 tbs brandy	1 tbs brandy
1x5ml/1 tsp mustard	1 tsp mustard
salt, white pepper	salt, white pepper
8 walnut halves	8 walnut halves
8 lettuce leaves	8 lettuce leaves

Drain the pears and sprinkle them with lemon juice.
Mix the cheese with the mayonnaise and beat in the brandy, mustard, salt and pepper. Spoon this mixture into a piping bag and pipe it into the pear halves. Top each one with a walnut half. Divide the lettuce leaves between 4 small plates, place two stuffed pears on each, and chill until serving.

CANAPÉS

Canapés are not intended to provide a meal but are an elegant accompaniment to drinks. They need a lot of time and patience to prepare: at least 3 hrs. to make enough for 12–15 guests. Allow about 4–5 canapés per person. The following quantities are enough for 8 people.

Salami with olives
Butter and quarter a slice of white bread with crusts removed and top each quarter with 2 small slices of salami. Garnish with sliced olives and onion rings.

Caviare with egg
Butter and quarter a slice of white bread with crusts removed and spread with caviare. Top each piece with a slice of hardboiled egg and some dill.

Asparagus tips with prawns
Butter and quarter a slice of white bread with crusts removed. Top with a lettuce leaf, tinned asparagus tips, prawns and a little parsley.

Chicken with mandarin oranges
Butter and quarter a slice of white bread with crusts removed. Top with sliced cooked chicken breast, mandarin oranges, walnut halves and parsley.

Steak Tartare with anchovies
Butter and quarter a slice of white bread with crusts removed. Spread with seasoned steak tartare. Garnish with cocktail onions, capers, and an anchovy roll.

Smoked salmon with egg
Cover the buttered and quartered slice of bread with sliced smoked salmon and garnish with wedges of hardboiled egg and dill.

Tongue with mushrooms
Butter and quarter a slice of white bread with crusts removed and top each quarter with 2 rolls of cooked tongue. Garnish with sliced mushrooms and parsley.

Roquefort cream
Cut a slice of white bread with crusts removed in quarters. Beat some Roquefort cheese with butter until creamy. Pipe on to the bread quarters and garnish with sliced radishes and cress.

COCKTAIL DIP FOR PRAWNS

Preparation time: 15 mins.
About 105 calories/440 joules

Metric/Imperial	American
200g/6 oz tomato ketchup	¾ cup tomato ketchup
3x5ml/3 tsp lemon juice	3 tsp lemon juice
2x5ml/2 tsp grated horseradish	2 tsp grated horseradish
2½ml/½ tsp salt	½ tsp salt
pinch of sugar	pinch of sugar
pinch of cayenne pepper	pinch of cayenne pepper
pinch of garlic powder	pinch of garlic powder
1 small lettuce	1 small lettuce
20 large prawns	20 large shrimps

Mix the tomato ketchup with lemon juice, horseradish, salt, sugar, cayenne pepper, and garlic powder and place in a small serving bowl. Cover a serving dish with lettuce leaves, place the dip in the centre, and arrange the prawns around it.

CHEESE DIP

Preparation time: 25 mins.
About 385 calories/1611 joules

Metric/Imperial	American
250g/8 oz cream cheese	½ lb cream cheese
50g/2 oz mayonnaise	¼ cup mayonnaise
2x15ml/2 tbs soured cream	2 tbs sour cream
salt, white pepper	salt, white pepper
2x5ml/2 tsp paprika	2 tsp paprika
2x5ml/2 tsp curry powder	2 tsp curry powder
few sprigs parsley	few sprigs parsley
4 sprigs fresh or 1 tsp dried dill	4 sprigs fresh or 1 tsp dried dill
few sprigs chives	few sprigs chives
small punnet cress	small punnet cress

This dip is particularly delicious when eaten with chicory leaves, tomato wedges, cheese biscuits, new potatoes, pretzels, cucumber sticks.
Sieve the cream cheese and stir in the mayonnaise and soured cream. Season with salt and pepper. Divide into 3 portions. Stir the paprika into the 1st portion and the curry powder into the 2nd portion. For the 3rd portion, finely chop all the herbs and stir into the cheese.

Attractively served, savoury cheese bites make a tasty snack for guests and family alike.

SAVOURY CHEESE BITES

Cheesy dates
Remove the stones from fresh dates. Beat some blue cheese with butter until creamy and pipe it into the dates. Place each one on a small lettuce leaf and serve with a cocktail stick.

Camembert discs
Cut white bread into rounds and spread them with butter. Top each with a wedge of Camembert cheese and a gherkin fan. Garnish with cress.

Party bites
Butter rounds of pumpernickel bread and cover with mixed pickles and strips of Emmenthal cheese. Top with gherkins wrapped in ham and pimento peppers. Garnish with parsley and serve with cocktail sticks.

Anchovy bites
Spread rounds of pumpernickel bread with herb cream cheese and cover with sliced hardboiled egg and tomato. Top with anchovy rolls, lumpfish roe and parsley.

Stuffed tomatoes
Beat some processed cheese spread with cream and finely chopped gherkin until creamy. Pipe into hollowed out tomatoes and garnish with parsley, radish slices, and paprika.

Cheese balls
Beat some processed cheese spread until smooth. With damp hands form into balls and roll in crumbled pumpernickel bread and paprika. Fasten on to cheese biscuits with cocktail sticks.

Salmon rolls
Place strips of Brie cheese on slices of smoked salmon, and roll them up. Garnish each with ½ a thin lemon slice, and fasten on to a buttered round of white bread with a cocktail stick.

Cheese cubes
Cut Gouda or Edam cheese into even cubes and fasten 1-2 stuffed olives on to each cheese cube with a cocktail stick.

NOTE:
For these savoury cheese bites, you can use almost any type of cheese, but be careful when using strong cheeses as they could easily be too overpowering.

WINDSOR CHICKEN SALAD

Preparation time: 1 hr.
About 410 calories/1716 joules

Metric/Imperial	American
4 chicken legs	4 chicken legs
salt	salt
60g/2½ oz butter	⅓ cup butter
125ml/4 fl oz chicken stock	½ cup chicken stock
150g/5 oz mushrooms	2½ cups mushrooms
2 celery sticks	2 celery sticks
1 gherkin	1 gherkin
pepper	pepper
3x15ml/3 tbs mayonnaise	3 tbs mayonnaise
2x5ml/2 tsp grated horseradish	2 tsp grated horseradish
1x5ml/1 tsp Worcester sauce	1 tsp Worcester sauce
pinch of sugar	pinch of sugar
2x15ml/2 tbs oil	2 tbs oil
1x15ml/1 tbs lemon juice	1 tbs lemon juice
salt, white pepper	salt, white pepper
pinch of sugar	pinch of sugar
lettuce for garnish	lettuce for garnish

Whether or not Windsor chicken salad was devised for the Royal Family is not known. The taste, however, is truly fit for a king.

Sprinkle the chicken legs with salt and fry them in melted butter until golden all over. Add the chicken stock, cover, and simmer for 20 mins. Meanwhile, trim and slice the mushrooms thinly. Dice the celery and the gherkin. Take the chicken legs out of the pan and remove the skin and bones. Leave to cool. Reheat the liquid remaining in the pan and cook the mushrooms for 5 mins. stirring frequently. Season lightly, drain and cool.

Cut the chicken flesh in 3cm/1 in. strips and add it to the mushrooms with the celery and gherkin. Mix the mayonnaise with the horseradish and Worcester sauce and season with salt and sugar. Stir into the chicken mixture. Cover and chill in the refrigerator for 10 mins. Make a dressing with the oil, lemon juice, salt, pepper, and sugar. Arrange the chicken salad in the centre of a large serving dish, surround with lettuce leaves and sprinkle over the dressing. Serve immediately.

Serve with bread and butter as a starter or light lunch dish.

BUDAPEST SALAD

Preparation time: 40 mins.
About 271 calories/1134 joules

Metric/Imperial	American
250g/8 oz cooked, lean beef	½ lb cooked, lean beef
2 red peppers	2 red peppers
2 tomatoes	2 tomatoes
1 onion	1 onion
For the dressing:	
1 clove garlic, salt	1 clove garlic, salt
3x15ml/3 tbs oil	3 tbs oil
2x15ml/2 tbs vinegar	2 tbs vinegar
pepper	pepper
few sprigs parsley	few sprigs parsley
3 lettuce leaves	3 lettuce leaves

Roughly dice the beef, red peppers, tomatoes and onion and mix all together in a bowl. Crush the garlic with a little salt, add the oil, vinegar, pepper and salt and mix well. Pour over the salad and leave to marinade for 30 mins. Sprinkle with chopped parsley. Arrange the salad on a serving dish lined with lettuce leaves.

Serve with white or brown bread and butter.

A salad fit for a king: Windsor chicken salad.

A tasty salad for slimmers: Budapest salad made with lean beef, red peppers, and tomatoes.

GRAPEFRUIT AND HAM SALAD

Preparation time: 35 mins.
About 425 calories/1779 joules

Metric/Imperial	American
200g/6 oz cooked ham	6 oz cooked ham
2 eating apples	2 eating apples
2 grapefruit	2 grapefruit
4 tinned pineapple slices	4 canned pineapple slices
100g/4 oz button mushrooms	4 oz mushrooms
3 tomatoes	3 tomatoes
8 stuffed green olives	8 stuffed green olives
For the dressing:	
3x15ml/3 tbs oil	3 tbs oil
2x15ml/2 tbs lemon juice	2 tbs lemon juice
salt, pepper	salt, pepper
pinch of sugar	pinch of sugar
For the garnish:	
2x15ml/2 tbs chopped nuts	2 tbs chopped nuts

Remove any fat from the ham and cut it in 3cm/1 in. strips. Peel, core and finely slice the apples. Halve the grapefruit and scoop out the flesh. Cut it into bite-size pieces. Drain the pineapple and cut into cubes. Cook the mushrooms and cool. Skin and quarter the tomatoes. Mix all these ingredients with the olives in a large bowl. For the dressing, mix together the oil, lemon juice, salt, pepper and sugar. Pour over the salad, cover and leave it to marinade in the refrigerator for 15 mins. Serve garnished with chopped nuts.

Grapefruit and ham salad.

Fish salad.

Japanese egg salad with tuna fish, mandarin oranges, and olives.

FISH SALAD

Preparation time: 35 mins.
About 455 calories/1904 joules

Metric/Imperial	American
500g/1 lb fillet of fish	1 lb fillet of fish
juice ½ lemon	juice ½ lemon
250ml/8 fl oz water, salt	1 cup water, salt
3 tomatoes	3 tomatoes
100g/4 oz tinned asparagus tips	4 oz canned asparagus tips
50g/2 oz halved walnuts	½ cup halved walnuts
For the sauce:	
1 egg yolk	1 egg yolk
1x5ml/1 tsp English mustard	1 tsp English mustard
100g/4 oz mayonnaise	½ cup mayonnaise
75g/3 oz natural yogurt	⅓ cup natural yogurt
salt	salt
pinch of sugar	pinch of sugar
white pepper	white pepper
125ml/4 fl oz soured cream	½ cup sour cream
For the garnish:	
1 lettuce	1 lettuce
1 tomato	1 tomato
1 hardboiled egg	1 hardboiled egg
few sprigs parsley	few sprigs parsley

Rinse the fish under cold water, pat dry and sprinkle with lemon juice. Bring the water with the salt to the boil, add the fish, reduce the heat and poach gently for 10 mins. Remove from the heat and cool the fish in the liquor for about 30 mins. Drain and break the fillet into bite-size pieces. Skin and quarter the tomatoes and mix them with the fish, together with the drained asparagus tips and walnut halves.

For the sauce, mix the egg yolk with the mustard and mayonnaise. Add the yogurt and season well with salt, pepper, and sugar. Stir in the soured cream. Reserve 2x15ml/2 tbs of the sauce and carefully fold the remainder into the salad. Leave to marinade for 10 mins. Line a flat serving dish with the washed lettuce leaves and pile the fish salad on top. Cover with the remaining sauce. Garnish with tomato and egg wedges and parsley.

Serve with fresh bread and butter as a lunch or supper dish, or with melba toast as a starter.

NOTE
Chopped walnuts could also be added to the garnish.

JAPANESE EGG SALAD

Preparation time: 20 mins.
About 355 calories/1485 joules

Metric/Imperial	American
200g/6 oz tinned tuna fish	6 oz canned tuna fish
4 hardboiled eggs	4 hardboiled eggs
200g/6 oz tinned mandarin oranges	6 oz canned mandarin oranges
50g/2 oz stuffed green olives	⅓ cup stuffed green olives
For the dressing:	
2x15ml/2 tbs lemon juice	2 tbs lemon juice
2x15ml/2 tbs soya sauce	2 tbs soya sauce
2x15ml/2 tbs oil	2 tbs oil
salt, pepper	salt, pepper
pinch of sugar	pinch of sugar
few sprigs parsley for garnish	few sprigs parsley for garnish

Drain and flake the tuna fish. Slice the eggs. Drain the mandarin oranges and olives and slice the olives. Mix all the ingredients lightly together.

For the dressing, stir the lemon juice and soya sauce into the oil and season with salt, pepper, and sugar. Pour over the salad and leave to marinade in the refrigerator for 10 mins. Divide the salad between 4 glass dishes and garnish with sprigs of parsley.

GRUYÈRE CUCUMBER SALAD

Preparation time: 30 mins.
About 320 calories/1339 joules

Metric/Imperial	American
150g/5 oz Gruyère cheese	1½ cups Gruyère cheese
75g/3 oz frozen prawns	3 oz frozen shrimps
1 small cucumber	1 small cucumber
For the dressing:	
4x15ml/4 tbs mayonnaise	4 tbs mayonnaise
2x15ml/2 tbs natural yogurt	2 tbs natural yogurt
2x5ml/2 tsp tomato ketchup	2 tsp tomato catsup
salt, white pepper	salt, white pepper
pinch of sugar	pinch of sugar
1x5ml/1 tsp lemon juice	1 tsp lemon juice
few sprigs dill	few sprigs dill

Defrost the prawns and place them in a bowl. Cut the cheese into narrow strips. Peel and thinly slice the cucumber and stir into the cheese and prawns. For the dressing, mix the mayonnaise with the yogurt and tomato ketchup and season with salt, pepper, sugar, and lemon juice. Add the chopped dill and fold into the salad mixture. Marinade for 20 mins. before serving.

GOAT'S CHEESE SALAD

Preparation time without chilling: 25 mins.
About 530 calories/2218 joules

Metric/Imperial	American
375g/12 oz goat's cheese	¾ lb goat's cheese
freshly ground black pepper	freshly ground black pepper
4x15ml/4 tbs olive oil	4 tbs olive oil
2x15ml/2 tbs white wine vinegar	2 tbs white wine vinegar
4 sticks celery	4 sticks celery
50g/2 oz pecan nuts, shelled	½ cup pecan nuts, shelled
salt	salt

Thinly slice the cheese and place it in a flat dish. Sprinkle generously with black pepper. Pour over 2x15ml/2 tbs of oil and 1x15ml/1 tbs of vinegar. Wash and trim the celery and slice it thinly. Sprinkle it over the cheese. Add the pecan nuts and remaining oil and vinegar. Season with salt, cover, and marinade in the refrigerator for 1 hr.

Serve with fresh bread for lunch or supper.

NOTE

If pecan nuts are not available, use halved walnuts instead.

TIP

Goat's cheese also goes very well with vine leaves, or fennel; but if using these, leave it to marinade longer.

Goat's cheese salad with celery and nuts.

GREEN BEAN, CUCUMBER, AND TOMATO SALAD

Preparation time: 45 mins.
85 calories/356 joules

Metric/Imperial	American
250g/8 oz green beans	½ lb green beans
250g/8 oz cucumber	½ lb cucumber
250g/8 oz tomatoes	½ lb tomatoes
For the dressing:	
2x15ml/2 tbs vinegar	2 tbs vinegar
salt, pepper	salt, pepper
1 onion, diced	1 onion, diced
1 large pinch of paprika	1 large pinch of paprika
pinch of garlic salt	pinch of garlic salt
4x15ml/4 tbs oil	4 tbs oil
few sprigs parsley for garnish	few sprigs parsley for garnish

Trim the beans and cook them in boiling, salted water until tender. Drain and cool. Slice the cucumber and tomatoes. Make a dressing of the remaining ingredients. Layer the cucumber and tomato slices in a glass serving dish or in 4 individual dishes, and top with the beans. Pour the dressing over and leave to marinade for 30 mins. Garnish with parsley and serve.

BROAD BEAN SALAD

Preparation time without marinading: 15–45 mins.
(including boiling fresh beans)
329 calories/1377 joules

Metric/Imperial	American
500g/8 oz tinned broad beans or 1kg/2¼ lbs fresh in their pods	½ lb canned lima beans or 2¼ lbs fresh in their pods
salt	salt
2x15ml/2 tbs vinegar, salt	2 tbs vinegar, salt
pinch of sugar	pinch of sugar
pinch of paprika	pinch of paprika
4x15ml/4 tbs oil	4 tbs oil
1 onion, diced	1 onion, diced
125g/4 oz streaky bacon	6 fatty bacon slices

Drain the beans and season them lightly with salt (shell fresh beans and cook them in boiling water for about 30 mins. until tender). Make a dressing with the vinegar, salt, sugar, paprika, oil, and onion. Stir in the beans and leave them to marinade for at least 1 hr. Fry the bacon until crisp, crumble it and stir it into the bean salad.

HUNGARIAN BEAN SALAD

Preparation time without soaking or chilling:
1 hr. 45 mins.
213 calories/892 joules

Metric/Imperial	American
250g/8 oz dried haricot beans	½ lb dried navy beans
salt	salt
2 red peppers	2 red peppers
¼ white cabbage, shredded	¼ white cabbage, shredded
1 onion, diced	1 onion, diced
For the dressing:	
2x15ml/2 tbs white wine vinegar	2 tbs white wine vinegar
salt, paprika	salt, paprika
garlic salt	garlic salt
4x15ml/4 tbs sunflower oil	4 tbs sunflower oil

Soak the beans in water overnight and then cook them in boiling, salted water until tender. Drain. Halve, seed, and slice the peppers thinly, and mix them with the beans, cabbage, and onion. Stir the vinegar, salt, paprika, garlic salt, and oil together and season well. Pour over the salad. Chill for 2–3 hrs.

TIP
If more salt is needed in the salad after it has been prepared, dissolve the salt in a little water and fold it into the salad. The salt disperses better this way.

CHICORY AND MANDARIN SALAD

Preparation time: 25 mins.
About 170 calories/711 joules

Metric/Imperial	American
4 heads of chicory	4 heads of Belgian endive
1 small tin of mandarin oranges	1 small can of mandarin oranges
For the dressing:	
4x15ml/4 tbs oil	4 tbs oil
2x15ml/2 tbs mandarin syrup	2 tbs mandarin syrup
juice ½ lemon	juice ½ lemon
2½ml/½ tsp celery salt	½ tsp celery salt
1 large pinch of dried thyme	1 large pinch of dried thyme
white pepper	white pepper
For the garnish:	
1 orange	1 orange
1 punnet cress	1 punnet cress

Wash and trim the chicory, cut about 1cm/½in. off the root ends and remove the bitter cores. Wash again, drain, and cut into rings. Drain the mandarin oranges, reserving the juice, and mix with the chicory.
For the dressing, stir the oil, mandarin syrup, and lemon juice together and season with celery salt, thyme, and pepper. Pour over the salad and marinade for 10 mins. Serve garnished with slices of orange and cress.

WHITE BEAN SALAD

Preparation time without soaking and marinading:
1 hr. 15 mins.
475 calories/1988 joules

Metric/Imperial	American
300g/10 oz dried haricot beans	10 oz dried navy beans
salt	salt
100g/4 oz mayonnaise or tartare sauce	½ cup mayonnaise or tartare sauce
1x15ml/1 tbs barbecue or tomato sauce	1 tbs barbecue or tomato sauce
pepper	pepper
1 pinch of sugar	1 pinch of sugar
few sprigs parsley	few sprigs parsley
1 tomato	1 tomato

Soak the beans overnight and cook them in boiling, salted water for about 70 mins. until tender. Drain well. Mix the mayonnaise with the barbecue sauce, salt, pepper, and sugar and stir into the beans. Leave to marinade for 2–3 hrs. Taste for seasoning and serve garnished with parsley and tomato wedges.

COSTA RICAN SALAD

Preparation time: 15 mins.
128 calories/536 joules

Metric/Imperial	American
4 tomatoes	4 tomatoes
3 bananas	3 bananas
juice 1 lemon	juice 1 lemon
2x15ml/2 tbs olive oil	2 tbs olive oil
salt, black pepper	salt, black pepper
curry powder	curry powder
few sprigs chives	few sprigs chives
a little cress	a little cress

Skin and slice the tomatoes. Peel and slice the bananas and sprinkle them with a little lemon juice. Arrange the tomato and banana slices attractively on a flat serving dish. Make a dressing of lemon juice, olive oil, salt, pepper, and curry powder and pour it over the salad. Sprinkle with snipped chives and cress.

TIP
Always sprinkle cut bananas with lemon juice to prevent them from discolouring.

SHEPHERDESS SALAD

Preparation time: 20 mins.
About 165 calories/690 joules

Metric/Imperial	American
For the sauce:	
60g/2½ oz Roquefort cheese	½ cup Roquefort cheese
125ml/4 fl oz single cream	½ cup light cream
1x15ml/1 tbs lemon juice	1 tbs lemon juice
salt, white pepper	salt, white pepper
In additon:	
8 lettuce hearts	8 lettuce hearts
1x15ml/1 tbs chopped fresh or 1x5ml/1 tsp dried tarragon	1 tbs chopped fresh or 1 tsp dried tarragon
1x15ml/1 tbs chopped fresh or 1x5ml/1 tsp dried chervil	1 tbs chopped fresh or 1 tsp dried chervil

For the sauce, crumble the Roquefort with a fork and mix with the cream, lemon juice, salt, and pepper.

Wash and dry the lettuce hearts and cut each one in quarters. Divide them between 4 plates. Pour the sauce over and sprinkle with the chopped or dried herbs.

Serve with toast and butter.

A meal in itself: Milanese macaroni salad.

MILANESE MACARONI SALAD

Preparation time without chilling: 40 mins.
About 680 calories/2846 joules

Metric/Imperial	American
150g/5 oz macaroni	1¼ cups macaroni
100g/4 oz frozen peas	¼ lb frozen peas
1 onion	1 onion
1 red pepper	1 red pepper
100g/4 oz cooked tongue	¼ lb cooked tongue
100g/4 oz salami	¼ lb salami
1 gherkin	1 gherkin
5 slices Emmenthal cheese	5 slices Swiss cheese
For the dressing:	
100g/4 oz mayonnaise	½ cup mayonnaise
4x15ml/4 tbs milk	4 tbs milk
1x15ml/1 tbs lemon juice	1 tbs lemon juice
salt, white pepper	salt, white pepper
cayenne pepper	cayenne pepper
For the garnish:	
2 hardboiled eggs	2 hardboiled eggs
3 tomatoes	3 tomatoes
few sprigs parsley	few sprigs parsley

Cook the macaroni in boiling, salted water for 15 mins. until tender. Cook the peas in boiling, salted water until tender, then drain and cool them. Drain the macaroni, rinse it under cold water and drain it again. Finely chop the onion. Halve, seed and slice the pepper. Slice the tongue, salami, gherkin, and cheese and mix with the macaroni, peas, onion, and pepper. For the dressing, mix the mayonnaise with the milk, lemon juice, salt, pepper, and cayenne pepper and pour it over the salad. Stir lightly and chill in the refrigerator for 1 hr. Before serving, cut the eggs in wedges, quarter the tomatoes, and finely chop the parsley. Garnish the salad with a ring of egg and tomato wedges and sprinkle with parsley.

Shepherdess salad.

Fig fruit salad.

FIG FRUIT SALAD

Preparation time: 35 mins.
About 265 calories/1109 joules

Metric/Imperial	American
8 fresh figs	8 fresh figs
1 orange	1 orange
1 eating apple	1 eating apple
250g/8 oz strawberries, hulled	½ lb strawberries, hulled
250g/8 oz black grapes	½ lb black grapes
4x15ml/4 tbs caster sugar	4 tbs granulated sugar
juice 1 lemon	juice 1 lemon
3x15ml/3 tbs kirsch	3 tbs kirsch
50g/2 oz walnuts, chopped	½ cup walnuts, chopped
125ml/4 fl oz whipping cream	½ cup whipping cream
1x15ml/1 tbs vanilla sugar	1 tbs vanilla flavored sugar

Skin and quarter the figs. Peel the orange and divide it into segments. Peel, core, and slice the apple. Reserving a few strawberries and grapes for garnish, mix all the fruit in a bowl. Sprinkle with sugar and pour over the lemon juice and kirsch. Add all but a few of the walnuts, and leave the salad to marinade for 10 mins., before dividing it between 4 glass dishes. Whip the cream until stiff and fold in the vanilla sugar. Spoon it into a piping bag and decorate the salads with it. Top each with a few strawberries, grapes, and walnuts. Chill before serving.

BAHIA SALAD

Preparation time: 15 mins.
246 calories/1030 joules

Metric/Imperial	American
4 blood oranges	4 blood oranges
3 bananas	3 bananas
3x15ml/3 tbs caster sugar	3 tbs granulated sugar
4x15ml/4 tbs desiccated coconut	4 tbs shredded coconut
juice 1½ lemons	juice 1½ lemons

Serve the Bahia salad as a welcome refreshment on a hot summer's day.
Peel the oranges and divide them into segments. Slice the bananas. Layer the oranges and bananas in a glass bowl with the sugar and coconut. Sprinkle with lemon juice and chill well before serving.
Serve with whipped cream and sponge fingers.

Garda fruit salad is named after the beautiful Italian town of Garda.

GARDA FRUIT SALAD

Preparation time without chilling: 30 mins.
About 170 calories/711 joules

Metric/Imperial	American
250g/8 oz black grapes	½ lb black grapes
3 tart apples	3 tart apples
5 pickled green almonds	5 pickled green almonds
1x15ml/1 tbs vanilla sugar	1 tbs vanilla flavored sugar
3x15ml/3 tbs caster sugar	3 tbs granulated sugar
juice 1 lemon	juice 1 lemon
3x15ml/3 tbs brandy	3 tbs brandy

Halve and remove the pips from the grapes. Peel, core, and slice the apples. Finely slice the pickled almonds. Mix the fruit together in a bowl and sprinkle with vanilla sugar and caster sugar. Pour the lemon juice and brandy over. Stir well and chill for 1 hr before serving.

FREEZER FRUIT SALAD

Preparation time: 30 mins.

Metric/Imperial	American
500g/1 lb strawberries	1 lb strawberries
500g/1 lb redcurrants	1 lb redcurrants
500g/1 lb raspberries	1 lb raspberries
500g/1 lb bilberries	1 lb blueberries
500g/1 lb cherries	1 lb cherries
500g/1 lb sugar	1 lb sugar

Only use fruit which are ripe and without blemish. Wash and trim the fruit, and stone the cherries. Layer the fruit into freezer boxes, sprinkling with sugar as you go along. Seal the boxes and freeze for up to 12 mths.

To serve:
Defrost and serve with whipped cream. A little kirsch or any fruit liqueur, some sliced oranges or bananas could be added before serving.

Jamaican salad.

JAMAICAN SALAD

Preparation time: 30 mins.
About 440 calories/1841 joules

Metric/Imperial	American
2 bananas	2 bananas
juice 1 lemon	juice 1 lemon
2 oranges	2 oranges
1 grapefruit	1 grapefruit
200g/6 oz jar of stoned morello cherries	6 oz jar of stoned morello cherries
25g/1 oz hazelnuts, chopped	2 tbs hazelnuts, chopped
For the dressing:	
100g/4 oz mayonnaise	½ cup mayonnaise
juice ½ lemon	juice ½ lemon
pinch of salt	pinch of salt
2x15ml/2 tbs single cream	2 tbs light cream
1x15ml/1 tbs brandy	1 tbs brandy
sugar	sugar
25g/1 oz hazelnuts for garnish	2 tbs hazelnuts for garnish

Halve the bananas lengthwise and scoop out the flesh. Sprinkle the insides of the skins and flesh with lemon juice. Cube the banana flesh and place in a bowl. Peel the oranges and grapefruit and dice the flesh. Drain the cherries. Mix all the fruit together and sprinkle with chopped hazelnuts.

For the dressing, mix the mayonnaise with the lemon juice, salt, cream, brandy, and sugar, and pour over the fruit salad. Mix well and taste for seasoning. Spoon the fruit salad into the banana skins. Toast the hazelnuts, rub off the skins, chop roughly, and sprinkle over the salad. Serve immediately.

Serve as part of a cold buffet, a party snack, or as a starter.

GARLIC SOUP WITH GRAPES

Preparation time: 40 mins.
About 305 calories/1276 joules

Metric/Imperial	American
25g/1 oz butter	2 tbs butter
2 cloves garlic	2 cloves garlic
25g/1 oz flour	2 tbs flour
500ml/16 fl oz hot chicken stock	2 cups hot chicken stock
salt, white pepper	salt, white pepper
juice ½ lemon	juice ½ lemon
250ml/8 fl oz white wine	1 cup white wine
1x15ml/1 tbs madeira	1 tbs madeira
125ml/4 fl oz whipping cream	½ cup whipping cream
500g/1 lb black grapes	1 lb black grapes

Melt the butter in a saucepan. Finely chop the garlic and add to the butter. Sprinkle with flour and cook for 2 mins. Pour in the stock, stirring continuously. Season with salt, pepper, and lemon juice. Simmer for 5 mins. Pour in the white wine and madeira and heat through. Whip the cream and fold it in. Peel, halve and remove the pips from the grapes and add them to the soup. Serve hot.

Hamburg mussel soup makes a delicious starter for a gourmet meal.

HAMBURG MUSSEL SOUP

Preparation time: 1 hr. 40 mins.
About 825 calories/3453 joules

Metric/Imperial	American
2kgs/4½ lbs mussels	4½ lbs mussels
juice 1 lemon	juice 1 lemon
250ml/8 fl oz white wine	1 cup white wine
salt	salt
125g/4 oz smoked belly pork	¼ lb smoked belly pork
3 large onions	3 large onions
2 tomatoes	2 tomatoes
few sprigs parsley	few sprigs parsley
2 sticks celery	2 sticks celery
1 sprig fresh or 1¼ml/¼ tsp dried thyme	1 sprig fresh or ¼ tsp dried thyme
½ bay leaf	½ bay leaf
500ml/16 fl oz hot stock	2 cups hot stock
50g/2 oz butter	¼ cup butter
2x15ml/2 tbs plain flour	2 tbs all purpose flour
250ml/8 fl oz single cream	1 cup light cream
paprika	paprika

Carefully scrub the mussels under cold running water and place them in a large saucepan. Discard any opened mussels. Pour in the lemon juice and white wine and add salt. Bring to the boil and simmer for 10 mins. Drain the mussels, and reserve the liquor. Take the mussels out of their shells, removing the dark beards. Keep warm. Dice the belly pork and onions. Skin the tomatoes and cut off the stalk ends. Finely chop the parsley and slice the celery.

Fry the pork in a saucepan until the fat runs and add the onions. Cook for 10 mins. Add the tomatoes, parsley, celery, thyme, and bay leaf. Pour in the hot stock and mussel liquor, and bring to the boil. Simmer for 30 mins. and then rub through a strainer. Bring back to the boil.

Meanwhile, mix the butter with the flour to a smooth paste and gradually add to the soup, stirring continuously. Simmer for 5 mins. Remove from the heat and stir in the cream and the mussels. Season with paprika and salt if necessary.

NOTE

Some white part of leek, cut into strips, could be added with the butter and flour.

Lemon soup with white islands can be eaten hot or cold.

LEMON SOUP

Preparation time: 40 mins.
About 280 calories/1172 joules

Metric/Imperial	American
3 lemons	3 lemons
500ml/16 fl oz water	2 cups water
250ml/8 fl oz white wine	1 cup white wine
1 pinch of salt	1 pinch of salt
150g/5 oz sugar	2/3 cup sugar
25g/1 oz cornflour	2 tbs cornstarch
2 eggs	2 eggs
2x15ml/2 tbs vanilla sugar	2 tbs vanilla flavored sugar

Cook the lemons in boiling water for 10 mins. Pour through a sieve into a measuring jug. Press down on the lemons to extract all of the juice. Add the white wine and make up to 1 litre/1¾ pints/4½ cups with water. Return to the saucepan, add salt and 75g/3 oz/½ cup of the sugar and bring to the boil. Mix the cornflour with a little water and stir it into the soup. Bring to the boil and remove from the heat.

Separate the eggs. Beat the egg yolks with a little soup until blended and then stir them into the soup. Whip the egg whites until stiff and fold in the remaining sugar and vanilla sugar. With a teaspoon, form little balls of meringue mixture and place them on top of the soup. Cover the pan and simmer for 10 mins., but do not allow it to boil. Serve immediately.

Serve hot or cold as a starter or dessert.

ALMOND CHICKEN SOUP

Preparation time: 2 hr. 10 mins.
About 475 calories/1988 joules

Metric/Imperial	American
1 boiling chicken, 1kg/2¼ lb	1 boiling chicken, 2¼ lbs
1½ litres/2½ pints water salt	6¼ cups water, salt
2 sticks celery	2 sticks celery
2 carrots	2 carrots
100g/4 oz ground almonds grated nutmeg	1 cup ground almonds grated nutmeg
large pinch of cayenne pepper	large pinch of cayenne pepper
1x15ml/1 tbs sherry	1 tbs sherry
125ml/4 fl oz whipping cream	½ cup whipping cream

Cook the chicken in boiling, salted water for 1½ hrs. until tender. Meanwhile, roughly chop the celery and carrots and add to the chicken 30 mins. before the end of the cooking time. Take the chicken out of the pan and remove the skin and bones. Cut the flesh into bite-size pieces. Strain the stock and remove the fat if necessary. Return the chicken meat to the stock, add the ground almonds and season with nutmeg and cayenne pepper. Reheat and add the sherry. Whip the cream and lightly fold into the soup just before serving.

Chicory soup.

CHICORY SOUP

Preparation time: 35 mins.
About 305 calories/1276 joules

Metric/Imperial	American
500g/1 lb chicory	1 lb Belgian endive
75g/3 oz streaky bacon, diced	4 fatty bacon slices, diced
25g/1 oz butter or margarine	2 tbs butter or margarine
2 onions, chopped	2 onions, chopped
25g/1 oz flour	2 tbs flour
1 litre/1¾ pints hot stock	4½ cups hot stock
salt, nutmeg	salt, nutmeg
1 egg yolk	1 egg yolk
2x15ml/2 tbs soured cream	2 tbs sour cream
chopped parsley	chopped parsley

Wash and trim the chicory and cut off the root ends. Remove the cores and finely slice the remainder. Fry the bacon in the butter or margarine and add the copped onions. Stir in the chicory, sprinkle with flour, and pour in the stock. Simmer for 7 mins. Season with salt and nutmeg. Remove from the heat. Mix the egg yolk with the soured cream and stir into the hot soup. Do not allow it to boil. Sprinkle with chopped parsley and serve.

CROATIAN APPLE SOUP

Preparation time: 35 mins.
582 calories/2436 joules

Metric/Imperial	American
6 cooking apples	6 cooking apples
1x5ml/1 tsp ground cinnamon	1 tsp ground cinnamon
juice ½ lemon	juice ½ lemon
500ml/16 fl oz water	2 cups water
60g/2½ oz butter	⅓ cup butter
1x15ml/1 tbs flour	1 tbs flour
500ml/16 fl oz white wine	2 cups white wine
1x15ml/1 tbs sugar	1 tbs sugar
2x15ml/2 tbs white bread, cubed	2 tbs white bread, cubed

Peel and core the apples and cut them into cubes. Cook to a purée with the cinnamon, lemon juice, and water. Melt half the butter, add the flour, and cook for 1 min. stir in the white wine and sugar. Sieve the apple purée into the pan and bring to the boil. Melt the remaining butter and fry the bread cubes until golden brown. Garnish the soup with the croutons.

RUMP STEAK SURPRISE

Preparation time: 35 mins.
538 calories/2252 joules

Metric/Imperial	American
1 piece of rump steak weighing about 500g/18 oz	1 piece of rump steak weighing about 18 oz
150g/5 oz ham, finely chopped	1¼ cup ham, finely chopped
150g/5 oz mushrooms, sliced	1¼ cups mushrooms, sliced
2 onions	2 onions
few sprigs parsley	few sprigs parsley
1x15ml/1 tbs chopped fresh or 1x5ml/ 1 tsp crumbled dried chervil	1 tbs chopped fresh or 1 tsp crumbled dried chervil
salt, white pepper	salt, white pepper
100g/4 oz lean minced beef	1 cup lean ground beef
1 egg yolk	1 egg yolk
4x15ml/4 tbs oil	4 tbs oil

With a sharp knife make a horizontal cut in the steak to produce a pocket. Finely chop one onion and mix with the chopped ham and mushrooms. Add the finely chopped parsley and chervil and season with salt and pepper. Finely chop the second onion and mix with the minced beef, egg yolk, salt and pepper. First stuff the steak with the beef mixture and then with the ham mixture. Close the opening and secure with wooden cocktail sticks. Heat the oil in a frying pan until smoking and fry the steak briefly on both sides to seal in the juices. Reduce the heat and continue cooking the steak for about 15 mins. until done. The stuffed steak will take a little longer to cook because of its thickness.

Picture on pages 52/53: rump steak surprise.

BEEF STROGANOFF

Preparation time: 25 mins.
559 calories/2340 joules

Metric/Imperial	American
50g/2 oz margarine or oil	¼ cup margarine or oil
3 onions, sliced	3 onions, sliced
250g/8 oz mushrooms, sliced	½ lb mushrooms, sliced
salt, sugar	salt, sugar
1x15ml/1 tbs mustard	1 tbs mustard
black pepper	black pepper
750g/1½ lbs fillet of beef	1½ lbs fillet of beef
50g/2 oz margarine	¼ cup margarine
250ml/8 fl oz soured cream	1 cup sour cream

This famous recipe for steak is named after the Stroganoffs, an important merchant family who were mainly involved in the commercial development of Siberia.

Heat the fat in a frying pan and add the sliced onions and mushrooms. Cook for 5 mins., then season with salt, sugar, mustard, and pepper. Cut the beef into strips about 5cm/2 in. long and 1cm/½ in. wide. Melt the margarine in a separate frying pan and quickly fry the meat for 5 mins. until brown on all sides. Add the meat to the vegetables. Stir in the soured cream and serve immediately.

TIP
Beef Stroganoff can also be prepared as follows: fry the meat for 2 mins., add the mushrooms and onions and fry for another 2 mins. Stir in the soured cream and seasonings.

BOEUF À LA MODE

Braised beef in red wine
Serves 6.

Preparation time without marinading: 3 hrs.
863 calories/3613 joules

Metric/Imperial	American
1kg/2¼ lbs rolled topside of beef	2¼ lbs rolled round of beef
salt, black pepper	salt, black pepper
For the marinade:	
700ml/1¼ pints red wine	3 cups red wine
250ml/8 fl oz water	1 cup water
1 onion, sliced	1 onion, sliced
1 carrot, sliced	1 carrot, sliced
1 clove garlic, crushed	1 clove garlic, crushed
1 bay leaf	1 bay leaf

Boeuf à la mode.

2x5ml/2 tsp parsley, chopped	2 tsp parsley, chopped
a little thyme	a little thyme
For braising:	
40g/1½ oz margarine	3 tbs margarine
50g/2 oz streaky bacon, diced	3 slices fatty bacon, diced
2x15ml/2 tbs brandy	2 tbs brandy
1 veal bone	1 veal bone
1 tomato	1 tomato
few sprigs parsley	few sprigs parsley
½ bay leaf	½ bay leaf
¼ leek	¼ leek
250ml/8 fl oz beef stock	1 cup beef stock
salt	salt
For the garnish:	
1x15ml/1 tbs margarine	1 tbs margarine
40g/1½ oz streaky bacon, diced	2 slices fatty bacon, diced
10 small onions	10 small onions
8 carrots, salt	8 carrots, salt
few sprigs parsley	few sprigs parsley

Preheat oven to 220°C/425°F/Gas 7 . Wipe the beef and season with salt and pepper. Mix the ingredients for the marinade together and immerse the meat in it until it is completely covered. Leave to marinade for 6 hrs at room temperature or overnight in the refrigerator. Turn the meat occasionally.

Drain the meat and wipe dry. Melt the margarine in a large pan and fry the diced bacon until golden. Add the meat and brown well on all sides. Pour in the brandy, ignite it, and flambé the meat. Add the veal bone, skinned and quartered tomato, chopped parsley, bay leaf, sliced leek, and stock to the pan. Sprinkle with salt. Strain the marinade and pour it over the meat. Cover and braise in the preheated oven on the centre shelf for 2 hrs.

While the meat is cooking, prepare the garnish. Heat the margarine and brown the diced bacon in it. Remove the bacon with a slotted spoon. Fry the whole onions and the carrots, cut into oval shapes, in the hot fat for about 30 mins. until tender and brown all over. Season lightly with salt.

Remove the meat from the oven and arrange it on a heated serving plate. Surround it with the onions, carrots, and parsley. Strain the braising liquor, remove the fat if necessary, and reduce it a little by boiling. Pour a little sauce over the meat and serve the rest separately.

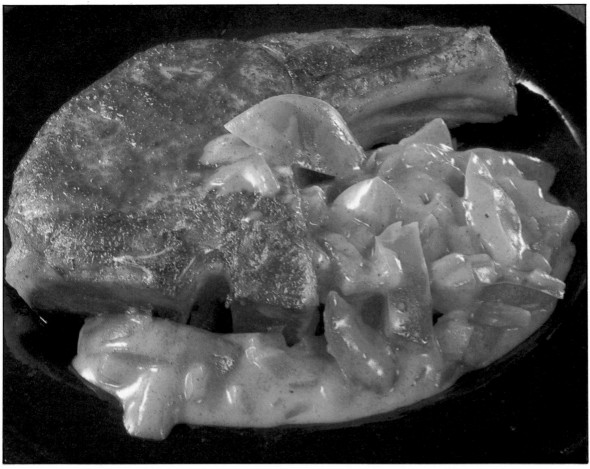

Hungarian pepper chops are simple to prepare but are very tasty.

HUNGARIAN PEPPER CHOPS

Preparation time: 40 mins.
About 590 calories/2469 joules

Metric/Imperial	American
4 pork chops, 150g/ 5 oz each	4 pork chops, 5 oz each
1 onion	1 onion
1 green pepper	1 green pepper
2 tomatoes	2 tomatoes
40g/1½ oz butter or margarine	3 tbs butter or margarine
salt, black pepper	salt, black pepper
paprika	paprika
250ml/8 fl oz hot water	1 cup hot water
1x5ml/1 tsp flour	1 tsp flour
3x15ml/3 tbs single cream	3 tbs light cream

Flatten the pork chops lightly with the palm of your hand and pat them dry with kitchen paper. Finely dice the onion. Halve, seed, and slice the pepper. Skin, seed, and slice the tomatoes thinly. Melt the butter or margarine in a frying pan and fry the pork chops for approx 6 mins. on each side until golden and cooked through. Season with salt, pepper, and paprika. Arrange them on a serving dish and keep warm. Fry the onion in the hot fat until golden, add the green pepper, and pour the water over. Cover and simmer for 2 mins. Add the tomatoes and simmer for a further 3 mins.

Blend the flour with a little water and thicken the sauce with it. Simmer for another 5 mins. Stir in the cream, taste for seasoning, and pour the sauce over the pork chops. Serve immediately.

DANISH PORK WITH APPLES

Pork Aebleflaesk

Preparation time: 1 hr 10 mins.
About 436 calories/1825 joules

Metric/Imperial	American
500g/1 lb loin of pork (or 4 chops)	1 lb loin of pork (or 4 chops)
salt, black pepper	salt, black pepper
2x15ml/2 tbs margarine	2 tbs margarine
2 onions, sliced	2 onions, sliced
2 apples, sliced	2 apples, sliced
parsley for garnish	parsley for garnish

Wipe the loin of pork and season with salt and pepper. Melt the margarine in a saucepan and fry the pork until brown on all sides. Pour in a little water and braise for about 1 hr, basting occasionally with the liquor. Ten mins. before the end of the cooking time, add the sliced onions and apples. Remove the meat and arrange it on a serving dish. Surround the pork with the apples and onions and garnish with parsley. If you are using pork chops, you only need to cook them for 10 mins. each side.

Danish pork with apples.

CANTONESE ROAST PORK

Preparation time: 1 hr. 50 mins.
About 525 calories/2197 joules

Metric/Imperial	American
1kg/2¼ lb leg of pork, boned and skinned	2¼ lb leg of pork, boned and skinned
1x15ml/1 tbs soya sauce	1 tbs soya sauce
2x15ml/2 tbs chicken stock	2 tbs chicken stock
1x15ml/1 tbs honey	1 tbs honey
1x15ml/1 tbs sugar	1 tbs sugar
salt	salt
1x5ml/1 tsp dayong (available in Chinese food markets)	1 tsp dayong (available in Chinese food markets)
2x15ml/2 tbs sesame or olive oil	2 tbs sesame or olive oi!

Preheat oven to 200°C/400°F/Gas 6. Rinse the pork under cold water and pat dry with kitchen paper. Mix the soya sauce, chicken stock, honey, sugar, salt, and dayong together and rub well into the pork. Cover the meat and leave it to marinade for 1 hr. Remove the pork from the marinade and drain. Place it in an ovenproof dish, and brush it all over with oil and some of the marinade. Cover, and cook in the preheated oven on the centre shelf for 1 hr. 20 mins.

Remove the meat from the oven and serve immediately in the dish.

Serve with boiled rice and bamboo shoots.

Joints are sometimes served in China, like this Cantonese roast pork.

Leg of lamb stuffed with kidneys and mushrooms.

STUFFED LEG OF LAMB

Serves 6.

Preparation time without soaking: 1 hr. 20 mins.
About 765 calories/3202 joules

Metric/Imperial	American
250g/8 oz lambs' kidneys	½ lb lambs' kidneys
250ml/8 fl oz milk	1 cup milk
25g/1 oz butter	2 tbs butter
150g/5 oz mushrooms	5 oz mushrooms
2½ml/½ tsp dried thyme	½ tsp dried thyme
2½ml/½ tsp dried rosemary	½ tsp dried rosemary
2½ml/½ tsp dried tarragon	½ tsp dried tarragon
salt, white pepper	salt, white pepper
6x15ml/6 tbs madeira	6 tbs madeira
1 leg of lamb, boned	1 leg of lamb, boned
2 cloves garlic	2 cloves garlic
3x15ml/3 tbs oil	3 tbs oil
250ml/8 fl oz hot meat stock	1 cup hot meat stock
1x5ml/1 tsp cornflour	1 tsp cornstarch

Soak the kidneys in the milk for 30 mins. Drain, dry, and dice them finely. Melt the butter and fry the kidneys for 5 mins. Slice the mushrooms and add them to the kidneys. Season with thyme, rosemary, tarragon, salt, and pepper. Pour in 4x15ml/4 tbs of madeira and simmer for 8 mins.

Meanwhile, rub the leg of lamb with the peeled garlic cloves and salt. Stuff the leg with the kidney mixture and sew up the opening with a strong thread. Heat the oil in a large pan and brown the meat all over for 15 mins. Pour in the stock, cover, and simmer for 45 mins.

Remove the thread from the meat and arrange it on a heated serving dish. Keep warm. Sieve the liquor into a saucepan. Blend the cornflour with the remaining madeira and thicken the gravy with it. Bring to the boil and serve immediately with the meat.

CROWN ROAST OF LAMB

Serves 6.

Preparation time: 2½ hrs.
About 1160 calories/4856 joules

Metric/Imperial

2 best ends of neck of
   lamb, 1kg/2¼ lbs each,
   chined
salt, garlic salt
black pepper
375ml/12 fl oz hot stock
125ml/4 fl oz white wine
300g/10 oz green beans
1 onion
25g/1 oz butter
large pinch of dried sage

For the sauce:
250ml/8 fl oz hot stock
1x15ml/1 tbs flour
3x15ml/3 tbs cold water
75g/3 oz natural yogurt
salt, black pepper
For the garnish:
2 tomatoes

American

2 rib roasts of lamb,
   2¼ lbs each, chined

salt, garlic salt
black pepper
1½ cups hot stock
½ cup white wine
10 oz green beans
1 onion
2 tbs butter
large pinch of dried
   sage

1 cup hot stock
1 tbs flour
3 tbs cold water
⅓ cup natural yogurt
salt, black pepper

2 tomatoes

Preheat oven to 180°C/350°F/Gas 4. Have the butcher chine and skin the lamb. Bend the necks of lamb into a crown shape and tie them together securely. Rub with salt, garlic salt, and pepper. Place the meat in a roasting tin, pour over the stock and wine and cover with aluminium foil. Roast in the preheated oven on the centre shelf for 2 hrs. Remove the foil after 1 hr.

Meanwhile, cook the beans in boiling, salted water for 15 mins. until tender. Drain. Finely chop the onion, and fry it in the butter for 5 mins. until golden. Add the beans and season with sage. Cover and keep warm. Take the meat out of the oven and remove the string. Arrange it on a heated serving dish and keep warm.

For the sauce, bring the juice in the roasting tin to the boil and add the stock. Mix the flour with a little water and add to the gravy to thicken it. Simmer for 5 mins. Stir in the yogurt and season with salt and pepper. Keep warm. Spoon the beans into the centre of the lamb crown and surround it with wedges of tomato. Serve immediately, accompanied by the sauce.

Serve with roast or croquet potatoes.

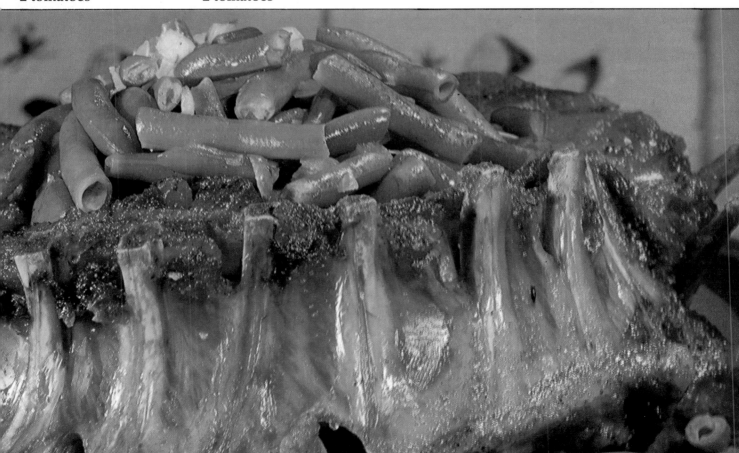

For all lovers of lamb: crown roast of lamb filled with green beans.

Simple but elegant: veal cutlets with herbs.

LAMB CUTLETS PROVENÇAL

Preparation time: 45 mins.
About 475 calories/1988 joules

Metric/Imperial	American

8 lamb cutlets,
  75g/3 oz each
	8 lamb cutlets,
	  3 oz each

salt, black pepper	salt, black pepper
3x15ml/3 tbs oil	3 tbs oil
2 onions	2 onions
1 clove garlic	1 clove garlic
2 green peppers	2 green peppers

400g/14 oz tinned
  tomatoes
	14 oz canned
	  tomatoes

Wipe the cutlets with kitchen paper and flatten them lightly with the palm of your hand. Chine the fat around the edges. Rub the cutlets with salt and pepper. Heat 1x15ml/1 tbs of the oil in a large frying pan and fry the cutlets for 5 mins. on each side until they are well browned. Remove them from the pan and keep warm.

Finely chop the onions and garlic. Seed the peppers and slice them thinly. Heat the remaining oil in the pan, and fry the onions, garlic, and peppers for 5 mins. Place the lamb cutlets on top and cover them with the tomatoes. Cover the pan and cook for 10 mins. Remove the lid and cook for a further 5 mins. so that most of the liquid evaporates. Season with salt and pepper and serve immediately

VEAL CUTLETS WITH HERBS

Preparation time: 40 mins.
About 445 calories/1863 joules

Metric/Imperial	American
4 veal cutlets, 200g/6 oz each	4 veal cutlets, 6 oz each
salt, white pepper	salt, white pepper
2x15ml/2 tbs flour	2 tbs flour
100g/4 oz butter	½ cup butter
125ml/4 fl oz white wine	½ cup white wine
few sprigs parsley	2 sprigs parsley
3 sprigs chervil	3 sprigs chervil
3 sprigs tarragon	3 sprigs tarragon
125ml/4 fl oz hot stock	½ cup hot stock
For the garnish:	
few sprigs parsley	few sprigs parsley
2 tomatoes	2 tomatoes

Pat the veal cutlets dry with kitchen paper and flatten them lightly with the palm of your hand. Season them with salt and pepper, and roll them in flour. Melt half the butter in a frying pan and fry the cutlets for 5 mins. each side until golden. Arrange them on a serving plate and keep warm. Pour the wine into the pan and bring to the boil. Finely chop the herbs and add to the boiling liquid. Add the stock and boil for about 15 mins. to reduce the sauce. Remove the pan from the heat and beat in the remaining butter with a wire whisk. Pour the sauce over the cutlets, and garnish with parsley sprigs and tomato wedges.

VEAL MARENGO

Preparation time: 55 mins.
About 305 calories/1276 joules

Metric/Imperial	American
750g/1½ lbs boneless veal	1½ lbs boneless veal
4x15ml/4 tbs oil and butter	4 tbs oil and butter
100g/4 oz onions	¼ lb onions
100g/4 oz mushrooms	¼ lb mushrooms
2 carrots	2 carrots
1x15ml/1 tbs tomato purée	1 tbs tomato paste
1 bay leaf	1 bay leaf
1x5ml/1 tsp chopped thyme	1 tsp chopped thyme
salt, white pepper	salt, white pepper
sugar	sugar
125ml/4 fl oz hot water	½ cup hot water
125ml/4 fl oz white wine	½ cup white wine
1x15ml/1 tbs flour	1 tbs flour
few sprigs parsley	few sprigs parsley
For the garnish:	
1x15ml/1 tbs sliced truffle	1 tbs sliced truffle
1 tomato	1 tomato

Cut the veal into cubes. Heat the fat in a saucepan and fry the meat for 10 mins. until it is browned on all sides. Remove from the pan and keep warm. Finely chop the onions and slice the mushrooms and carrots. Add to the pan and cook until soft. Stir in the tomato purée and season with bay leaf, thyme, salt, pepper, and a pinch of sugar. Pour in the water and wine and bring to the boil. Return the meat to the pan, cover, and simmer for 15 mins. Mix the flour with a little water, stir into the pan, and cook for a further 5 mins. Remove the bay leaf, finely chop the parsley and stir it in. Serve the veal marengo garnished with sliced truffle and wedges of tomato.

BURGUNDY ROULADES

Preparation time: 40 mins.
About 335 calories/1402 joules

Metric/Imperial	American
For the stuffing:	
100g/4 oz button mushrooms	4 oz mushrooms
1 onion	1 onion
25g/1 oz butter	2 tbs butter
salt, pepper	salt, pepper
1 pinch of lemon balm	1 pinch of lemon balm
1x5ml/1 tsp lemon juice	1 tsp lemon juice
In addition:	
4 thin slices lean boneless veal	4 thin slices lean boneless veal
25g/1 oz butter	2 tbs butter
margarine for greasing	margarine for greasing
75ml/3 fl oz white Burgundy	⅓ cup white Burgundy
250ml/8 fl oz single cream	1 cup light cream
½ a lettuce for garnish	½ a lettuce for garnish

Preheat oven to 220°C/425°F/Gas 7. Thinly slice the mushrooms and chop the onion. Melt the butter and cook the mushrooms and onion for 5 mins. Season with salt, pepper, lemon balm, and lemon juice. Flatten out the veal slices with the palm of your hand and spread the stuffing on top. Roll up and fasten the roulades with wooden cocktail sticks. Fry them in melted butter until they are lightly browned. Place them in a greased ovenproof dish and pour over the wine. Cover with the cream and cook in the preheated oven for 15 mins.

Remove the roulades from the oven and arrange them on the lettuce leaves. Pour over the juices and serve.

Burgundy roulades.

Chicken chasseur flambéed with mushrooms and shallots.

CHICKEN CHASSEUR

Preparation time: 1¾hrs.
About 685 calories/2867 joules

Metric/Imperial	American
4x15ml/4 tbs oil	4 tbs oil
2 poussins, 750g/ 1½ lbs each	2 baby chickens, 1½ lbs each
50g/2 oz butter	¼ cup butter
10 shallots	10 shallots
100g/4 oz mushrooms	¼ lb mushrooms
3x15ml/3 tbs cognac or brandy	3 tbs cognac or brandy
3x15ml/3 tbs white wine	3 tbs white wine
1x15ml/1 tbs tomato purée	1 tbs tomato paste
250ml/8 fl oz hot chicken stock	1 cup hot chicken stock
2x5ml/2 tsp dried tarragon	2 tsp dried tarragon
2x5ml/2 tsp dried chervil	2 tsp dried chervil
salt, black pepper	salt, black pepper

Heat the oil in a casserole dish and fry the poussins for about 10 mins. until golden all over. Add the butter and melt it. Peel the shallots and add them to the casserole. Brown them for 5 mins. Quarter the mushrooms and add them to the pan. Pour over the cognac or brandy, ignite it, and flambé the poussins. Pour in the white wine. Stir the tomato purée into the chicken stock and add to the sauce. Season with the herbs and salt and pepper. Cover and simmer for 40 mins. until the meat is cooked. Remove the poussins and cut them in half. Arrange them on a heated serving plate, pour over the sauce, and serve immediately.

PORTUGUESE CHICKEN

Preparation time: 1 hr. 35 mins.
About 670 calories/2804 joules

Metric/Imperial	American
1 roasting chicken, 1¼kgs/2½ lbs	1 broiler chicken, 2½ lbs
salt, white pepper	salt, white pepper
paprika	paprika
60g/2½ oz butter or margarine	⅓ cup butter or margarine
3 shallots	3 shallots
750g/1½ lbs tomatoes	1½ lbs tomatoes
few sprigs parsley	few sprigs parsley

Preheat oven to 200°C/400°F/Gas 6. Wipe the chicken inside and out with kitchen paper and rub all over with salt, pepper, and paprika. Melt ⅔ of the butter or margarine in an ovenproof casserole and fry the chicken for 5 mins. until golden all over. Cover the casserole, and place it in the preheated oven on the centre shelf for 1 hr.
After 45 mins. finely chop the shallots, and skin, seed, and chop the tomatoes. Melt the remaining butter in a frying pan and fry the shallots and tomatoes gently for 5 mins. stirring occasionally. Remove the casserole from the oven, add the tomato mixture, cover, and finish cooking in the oven. Finely chop the parsley and sprinkle over the chicken before serving. Serve the chicken in the covered casserole to retain all the flavours.
Serve with boiled rice or crusty bread.

*Portuguese chicken
served here
with whole tomatoes.*

Chicken breasts provençal.

CHICKEN BREASTS PROVENÇAL

Preparation time: 30 mins.
About 415 calories/1737 joules

Metric/Imperial	American
4 chicken breasts, boned	4 chicken breasts, boned
2x15ml/2 tbs oil	2 tbs oil
salt, white pepper	salt, white pepper
125ml/4 fl oz white wine	½ cup white wine
3 tomatoes	3 tomatoes
6 black olives	6 black olives
1 clove garlic	1 clove garlic
3x15ml/3 tbs hot water	3 tbs hot water
¼ chicken stock cube	¼ chicken stock cube
1x5ml/1 tsp flour	1 tsp flour
few sprigs parsley	few sprigs parsley

Pat the chicken breasts dry with kitchen paper. Heat the oil in a frying pan and fry the chicken for 1 min . on each side until brown, then continue frying for 15 mins. until tender. Season with salt and pepper. Arrange the chicken on a heated serving plate and keep warm. Pour the wine into the frying pan. Skin and chop the tomatoes. Stone the olives and slice them thinly. Add them to the pan with the tomatoes and crushed garlic. Pour in the hot water, and stir in the chicken stock cube. Mix the flour with a little cold water, stir into the sauce, and simmer for 5 mins.
Spread the tomato sauce over the chicken breasts and garnish with parsley.
Serve with a tomato salad and boiled rice.

INDIAN DUCK WITH PISTACHIOS

Preparation time: 3 hrs.
1895 calories/7932 joules

Metric/Imperial	American
1 oven-ready duck	1 oven-ready duck
salt	salt
1 day-old bread roll	1 day-old bread roll
250g/8 oz boiled rice	½ lb boiled rice
150g/5 oz pistachio nuts, finely chopped	1 cup pistachio nuts, finely chopped
1 piece of star anise	1 piece of star anise
2 small onions, grated	2 small onions, grated
150g/5 oz natural yogurt	⅔ cup natural yogurt
1 egg	1 egg
a little rosewater	a little rosewater
curry powder	curry powder
40g/1½ oz melted butter	3 tbs melted butter
1x5ml/1 tsp crushed peppercorns	1 tsp crushed peppercorns
For the garnish:	
1 lettuce leaf	1 lettuce leaf
1 tomato	1 tomato
few sprigs parsley	few sprigs parsley

Preheat the oven to 200°C/400°F/Gas 6. Wipe the duck with kitchen paper and sprinkle lightly with salt. Soak the bread roll in a little water, drain, and squeeze dry. Add it to the rice and pistachio nuts and stir in the crushed star anise, grated onions, yogurt, egg, rosewater, plenty of curry powder, and salt. Mix well and stuff the duck with this mixture. Sew up the opening and brush the duck with melted butter. Rub the skin well with the crushed peppercorns and place the duck in a roasting tin. Cook in the preheated oven for 1½–2 hrs.
From time to time, baste the duck with a little water and with more melted butter.
Arrange the duck on a heated serving plate and garnish with a lettuce leaf, tomato wedges, and parsley. Serve with the roasting juices.
Serve with boiled rice and preserved ginger.

Picture on facing page: kidneys in sherry sauce.

KIDNEYS IN SHERRY SAUCE

Metric/Imperial	American
750g/1½ lbs pigs' kidneys	1½ lbs pigs' kidneys
1 onion	1 onion
1 clove garlic	1 clove garlic
40g/1½ oz butter or margarine	3 tbs butter or margarine
1 bay leaf	1 bay leaf
4 cloves	4 cloves
250ml/8 fl oz hot chicken stock	1 cup hot chicken stock
salt	salt
black pepper	black pepper
1 pinch of sugar	1 pinch of sugar
1 pinch of grated nutmeg	1 pinch of grated nutmeg
paprika	paprika
3x15ml/3 tbs cornflour	3 tbs cornstarch
125ml/4 fl oz dry sherry	½ cup dry sherry

Preparation time: 35 mins.
About 360 calories/1506 joules

Skin the kidneys, if necessary. Halve them lengthwise and remove the cores and sinews. Soak them in water for about 1 hr., changing the water 2 or 3 times. Pat the kidneys dry with kitchen paper and slice them thickly. Finely chop the onion and garlic. Melt the butter or margarine in a saucepan and fry the onion and garlic for 3 mins. until transparent. Add the kidneys, bay leaf, and cloves and pour in the stock. Cover and simmer for 10 mins. Season with salt, pepper, sugar, nutmeg, and paprika. Remove the bay leaf and cloves from the sauce. Blend the cornflour with a little water and stir it into the kidney mixture. Bring to the boil. Stir in the sherry, reheat, but do not boil. Serve immediately in a heated serving dish.

JUTLAND GAMMON STEAKS

Preparation time: 50 mins.
About 810 calories/3390 joules

Metric/Imperial

4 gammon steaks,
   150g/5 oz each
white pepper
40g/1½ oz margarine
125ml/4 fl oz Hollandaise
   sauce
50g/2 oz Samsoe or
   Emmenthal cheese,
   grated
paprika
For the garnish:
3 onions
25g/1 oz butter
250g/8 oz mushrooms
juice ½ lemon
salt, white pepper
1x5ml/1 tsp cornflour
125ml/4 fl oz single cream
4 sprigs parsley
1 tomato

American

4 smoked ham steaks,
   5 oz each
white pepper
3 tbs margarine
½ cup Hollandaise
   sauce
½ cup Samsoe or Swiss
   cheese, grated

paprika

3 onions
2 tbs butter
½ lb mushrooms
juice ½ lemon
salt, white pepper
1 tsp cornstarch
½ cup light cream
4 sprigs parsley
1 tomato

Preheat oven to 220°C/425°F/Gas 7. Rinse the gammon steaks briefly under cold water and pat dry. Sprinkle them lightly with pepper.
Melt the margarine in a frying pan and fry the steaks gently for 8 mins. each side. Place the steaks in a shallow ovenproof dish. Mix the Hollandaise sauce with the cheese and spread this over the steaks. Sprinkle with paprika. Place the dish in the preheated oven on the top shelf, and cook for 10 mins.
For the garnish, finely chop the onions. Melt the butter and fry the onions for 5 mins. until transparent. Thinly slice the mushrooms and add to the onions. Fry for a further 5 mins. Season with lemon juice, salt, and pepper. Thicken the liquid with a little cornflour mixed with water. Stir in the cream, reheat, but do not boil. Garnish the browned gammon steaks with the mushroom mixture, sprigs of parsley, and wedges of tomato. Serve hot.

PLAICE WITH HERBS

Preparation time: 40 mins.
About 580 calories/2428 joules

Metric/Imperial

4 plaice, cleaned and
   gutted
juice 1 lemon
salt, white pepper
4x15ml/4 tbs ground
   almonds
75g/3 oz butter or
   margarine
few sprigs parsley
few sprigs dill
4 sprigs lemon balm
2 sprigs tarragon
2 eggs
125ml/4 fl oz single cream
25g/1 oz butter

American

4 plaice, cleaned and
   gutted
juice 1 lemon
salt, white pepper
4 tbs ground almonds

⅓ cup butter or
   margarine
few sprigs parsley
few sprigs dill
4 sprigs lemon balm
2 sprigs tarragon
2 eggs
½ cup light cream
2 tbs butter

Preheat oven to 200°C/400°F/Gas 6. Rinse the plaice under cold water and pat dry. Sprinkle both sides with lemon juice. Cover and leave for 15 mins. Season both sides of the fish with salt and pepper and roll them in the ground almonds. Melt the butter or margarine in a large frying pan and fry the plaice for 3 mins. each side. Remove the fish and place them in a greased, shallow, ovenproof dish. Finely chop the fresh herbs. Mix the eggs with the cream, add the chopped herbs and salt, and pour over the fish. Sprinkle over any remaining ground almonds and dot with butter. Place in the preheated oven on the centre shelf and cook for 15 mins. Serve hot.

Gourmets love Jutland gammon steaks.

Stuffed trout:
a delicacy reserved for
special occasions.

STUFFED TROUT

Preparation time: 1¼ hrs.
About 835 calories/3495 joules

Metric/Imperial	American
For the stuffing:	
200g/7 oz tinned lobster meat	7 oz canned lobster meat
25g/1 oz butter	2 tbs butter
2 onions, chopped	2 onions, chopped
1 egg	1 egg
2x5ml/2 tsp lemon juice	2 tsp lemon juice
salt, white pepper	salt, white pepper
few sprigs parsley	few sprigs parsley
few sprigs dill	few sprigs dill
2x15ml/2 tbs dried breadcrumbs	2 tbs dried breadcrumbs
In addition:	
4 trout, 250g/8 oz each	4 trout, ½ lb each
juice 1 lemon	juice 1 lemon
salt, white pepper	salt, white pepper
2x5ml/2 tsp hot mustard	2 tsp hot mustard
butter for greasing	butter for greasing
2 small shallots, chopped	2 small shallots, chopped
125ml/4 fl oz chablis	½ cup chablis French wine
For the garnish:	
8 puff pastry fleurons, ready cooked	8 puff paste fleurons, ready cooked
1x15ml/1 tbs butter	1 tbs butter
4 slices lemon	4 slices lemon

Preheat oven to 200°C/400°F/Gas 6. Flake the lobster meat but reserve a few nice red pieces for the garnish. Beat the butter in a bowl until light and fluffy and add the chopped onions and the egg. Stir in the lemon juice, salt, and pepper. Finely chop the parsley and dill and add to the mixture with the breadcrumbs. Mix well.

Clean the trout and rinse under cold water. Pat dry with kitchen paper. Sprinkle inside and out with lemon juice, salt, and pepper, and lightly rub with mustard. Stuff each trout generously with the filling. Butter an ovenproof dish and sprinkle the chopped shallots over the bottom. Cover them with any remaining stuffing. Place the trout on top, pour in the chablis, and cook in the preheated oven for 30 mins.

After 20 mins., place the puff pastry fleurons on a baking sheet and reheat them in the oven with the trout. Melt the butter, and quickly heat the reserved lobster pieces. Garnish the stuffed trout with the fleurons, the lobster and slices of lemon. Serve immediately.

BELGIAN CHICORY

Preparation time: 40 mins.
240 calories/1004 joules

Metric/Imperial	American
4 heads of chicory	4 head of Belgian endive
1x5ml/1 tsp butter or margarine	1 tsp butter or margarine
1x5ml/1 tsp lemon juice	1 tsp lemon juice
4 slices cooked ham	4 slices cooked ham
4 large slices Edam cheese	4 large slices Edam cheese
margarine for greasing	margarine for greasing
4 tomatoes	4 tomatoes
pepper	pepper
25g/1 oz butter	2 tbs butter
lettuce leaves for garnish	lettuce leaves for garnish

Preheat oven to 220°C/425°F/Gas 7. Wash and trim the chicory, removing the bitter core from the root end. Place in boiling, salted water, add the butter or margarine and lemon juice, and cook for 8–10 mins. until tender. Drain. Wrap each head first in a slice of ham and then in a slice of cheese. Place them in a greased ovenproof dish. Skin the tomatoes, cut them in half, and arrange them around the chicory rolls. Dot with butter and cook in a preheated oven for 15 mins.
Garnish with lettuce leaves and serve immediately.

TIP
Chicory is grown in the dark and therefore it must also be stored in the dark, as the leaves will soon turn green. It will keep for about a week in the refrigerator.

Double-baked potatoes.

DOUBLE-BAKED POTATOES

Preparation time: about 1½ hrs.
330 calories/1381 joules

Metric/Imperial	American
8 large potatoes	8 large potatoes
2x15ml/2 tbs oil	2 tbs oil
125ml/4 fl oz single cream	½ cup light cream
100g/4 oz Emmenthal cheese, grated	1 cup Swiss cheese, grated
salt, pepper	salt, pepper
nutmeg	nutmeg
paprika	paprika

Preheat oven to 200°C/400°F/Gas 6. Scrub the potatoes well under cold water and rub them with oil. Prick the skins several times with a fork and cook them in the preheated oven for 1–1¼ hrs.
Remove the baked potatoes from the oven and leave them to cool slightly. Then cut a slice off the top, and carefully remove the cooked potato flesh from the skins, leaving about ½cm/¼ in. all round. Mash the flesh with a fork and beat in the cream, grated cheese, salt, pepper, and nutmeg. Mix well to make a very creamy mixture. Spoon it into a piping bag and pipe it back into the potato shells. Pipe a little on the top, sprinkle with paprika, and return the potatoes to the oven for 5 mins.

Belgian chicory is wrapped in ham and cheese.

Savoury Sicilian vegetable hotpot.

SICILIAN VEGETABLE HOTPOT

Preparation time: 50 mins.
About 295 calories/1234 joules

Metric/Imperial	American
3 aubergines	3 eggplants
6 tomatoes	6 tomatoes
2 red and 2 green peppers	2 red and 2 green peppers
2 large onions	2 large onions
1 clove garlic	1 clove garlic
5x15ml/5 tbs olive oil	5 tsb olive oil
salt, cayenne pepper	salt, cayenne pepper
paprika	paprika
100g/4 oz green olives	¼ lb green olives
100g/4 oz black olives	¼ lb black olives
2 chillies in brine	2 chillies in brine
few sprigs parsley	few sprigs parsley

Cut off the stalk ends of the aubergines and tomatoes, scald with boiling water, skin, and dice the flesh. Halve, seed, and slice the peppers. Slice the onions and finely chop the garlic. Heat the oil in a saucepan and add the vegetables. Shake the pan gently to prevent burning. Season with salt, cayenne pepper, and paprika. Cover and simmer for 20 mins. Add a little water if necessary.
Stone and slice the olives. Drain and finely chop the chillies. Add both to the vegetables in the pan. Simmer for a further 10 mins. Sprinkle with chopped parsley and serve.

HUNGARIAN SAVOY CABBAGE

Preparation time: 55 mins.
About 380 calories/1590 joules

Metric/Imperial	American
1kg/2¼ lbs savoy cabbage	2¼ lbs savoy cabbage
150g/5 oz streaky bacon	7 fatty bacon slices
2 small onions	2 small onions
1x15ml/1 tbs paprika	1 tbs paprika
125ml/4 fl oz soured cream	½ cup sour cream
salt	salt

Quarter, trim, and shred the cabbage, discarding the stalk. Cook covered in boiling, salted water for 25 mins. until tender. Drain well. Dice the bacon and onions. Gently fry the bacon in a saucepan until the fat runs. Add the onions and fry for a further 6 mins. until golden. Stir occasionally. Add the cabbage, sprinkle with paprika, and cook for 2 mins. Stir in the soured cream and season with salt. Serve immediately.

RED CABBAGE WITH PINEAPPLE

Preparation time: 2 hrs.
About 365 calories/1527 joules

Metric/Imperial	American
1 red cabbage, about 1kg/2¼ lbs	1 red cabbage, about 2¼ lbs
2 cooking apples	2 cooking apples
75g/3 oz butter or margarine	⅓ cup butter or margarine
1 onion	1 onion
2 cloves	2 cloves
½ bay leaf	½ bay leaf
125ml/4 fl oz tinned pineapple juice	½ cup canned pineapple juice
125ml/4 fl oz red wine	½ cup red wine
salt, white pepper	salt, white pepper
2x15ml/2 tbs wine vinegar	2 tbs wine vinegar
For the garnish:	
25g/1 oz butter	2 tbs butter
3 slices tinned pineapple	3 slices canned pineapple

Remove the outer leaves from the red cabbage, quarter it, cut out the core, and shred it finely. Peel, core, and slice the apples.
Melt the butter or margarine in a saucepan and fry the cabbage and apples gently for 5 mins. Peel the onion, spike it with cloves and bay leaf, and add to the cabbage. Pour in the pineapple juice and red wine, season with salt and pepper and stir well. Cover the pan and gently braise the cabbage for 1½ hrs. Remove the onion and add the wine vinegar. Taste for seasoning.
For the garnish, melt the butter in a frying pan and fry the pineapple slices briefly until golden on both sides. Place the cabbage on a heated serving dish, and garnish with the pineapple.

CAULIFLOWER WITH MUSHROOMS

Preparation time: 1 hr. 20 mins.
About 350 calories/1465 joules

Metric/Imperial	American
1 cauliflower	1 cauliflower
250ml/8 fl oz milk	1 cup milk
250ml/8 fl oz water	1 cup water
1 packet instant mashed potato, enough for 500ml/16 fl oz	1 packet instant mashed potato, enough for 2 cups
salt, nutmeg	salt, nutmeg
1x15ml/1 tbs butter	1 tbs butter
For the mushroom topping:	
40g/1½ oz butter or margarine	3 tbs butter or margarine
40g/1½ oz flour	3 tbs flour
250g/8 oz button mushrooms	8 oz mushrooms
125ml/4 fl oz water	½ cup water
250ml/8 fl oz milk	1 cup milk
1 egg	1 egg
salt	salt
few sprigs parsley, finely chopped	few sprigs parsley, finely chopped

Preheat oven to 220°C/425°F/Gas 7. Wash and trim the cauliflower and soak for 30 mins. in salted water. Cook in fresh, salted, boiling water for 15 mins. Drain. For the potato purée, bring the milk and water to the boil. Beat in the instant potato and season with salt and nutmeg. Stir in the butter. Spread the mashed potato over the base of an ovenproof dish and place the cauliflower on top. Keep warm.
For the mushroom topping, melt the butter or margarine and stir in the flour. Chop the mushrooms and add to the pan. Pour in the water, and milk. Simmer for 5 mins. Take out a little of the sauce and stir it into the beaten egg. Return to the pan but do not allow it to boil. Season with salt, add the finely chopped parsley, and cover the cauliflower with the mushroom sauce. Place in the preheated oven on the centre shelf and cook for 15 mins.

NOTE
The potato purée could of course be made with fresh potatoes, but this takes a little longer.

Cauliflower with mushrooms:
an unusual vegetable accompaniment.

STUFFED AUBERGINE

Imam Bayildi

Preparation time: 45 mins.
About 180 calories/753 joules

Metric/Imperial	American
4 aubergines	4 eggplants
2x15ml/2 tbs oil	2 tbs oil
500g/1 lb tomatoes	1 lb tomatoes
25g/1 oz butter	2 tbs butter
100g/4 oz onions, sliced	¼ lb onions, sliced
2 cloves garlic, salt	2 cloves garlic, salt
1 bay leaf	1 bay leaf
1 cinnamon stick	1 cinnamon stick
white pepper	white pepper
several sprigs parsley	several sprigs parsley
margarine for greasing	margarine for greasing
6 black olives	6 black olives
6 anchovy fillets	6 anchovy fillets

The imam is the head of the Muslim community. Literally translated, this dish is called Fainted Imam. According to legend, there was once an imam in Constantinople who fainted with ecstasy on savouring a dish of aubergines, tomatoes, and onions. Since then, these aubergines have been called Imam Bayildi in Turkey.

Preheat oven to 180°C/350°F/Gas 4. Cut off the stalks of the aubergines. Heat the oil in a frying pan and fry the aubergines for about 5 mins. Remove them from the pan and skin them. Slit each one open lengthwise and carefully remove the flesh, taking care to leave a shell.

Skin and slice the tomatoes thinly. Melt the butter and fry the sliced onions for 5 mins. until golden. Add the tomatoes and cook for 10 mins. Crush the garlic with a little salt and add to the pan with the bay leaf, cinnamon stick, salt, and pepper. Finely chop the parsley and stir into the mixture. Simmer for a further 10 mins. Remove and discard the bay leaf and cinnamon stick. Spoon the stuffing into the aubergine shells and place them in a greased ovenproof dish. Bake in the preheated oven on the centre shelf for 10 mins.

Remove the dish from the oven and garnish with the olives and anchovy fillets rolled into rings. Serve hot or cold.

Serve with boiled rice and grilled lamb chops.

Savoury accompaniment to all kinds of fried or roast meat: onions in wine.

ONIONS IN WINE

Preparation time: 1 hr. 10 mins.
About 210 calories/879 joules

Metric/Imperial	American
750g/1½ lbs onions	1½ lbs onions
40g/1½ oz butter or margarine	3 tbs butter or margarine
salt, white pepper	salt, white pepper
large pinch of dried thyme	large pinch of dried thyme
juice ½ lemon	juice ½ lemon
pinch of sugar	pinch of sugar
1x15ml/1 tbs flour	1 tbs flour
250ml/8 fl oz white wine	1 cup white wine
few sprigs parsley	few sprigs parsley

Peel and slice the onions thickly. Heat the butter or margarine in a saucepan and fry the onion rings for 10 mins. until golden. Season with salt, pepper, thyme, lemon juice, and sugar. Sprinkle with the flour and cook gently for 2 mins. Stir in the white wine, cover and simmer gently for 25 mins. Place the onions in a heated serving bowl and sprinkle with chopped parsley.

Variation
Add a chopped clove of garlic to the onions or stir in 125ml/4 fl oz/½ cup soured cream at the end.

GREEN BEANS IN BATTER

Preparation time: 50 mins.
205 calories/858 joules

Metric/Imperial	American
250g/8 oz green beans	½ lb green beans
For the batter:	
75g/3 oz flour	¾ cup flour
2 eggs	2 eggs
a little milk, salt	a little milk, salt
oil for deep frying	oil for deep frying
parsley for garnish	parsley for garnish
1 lemon cut in wedges	1 lemon cut in wedges

Cook the beans in boiling, salted water for 15 mins. until just tender. Drain well. Mix the flour, eggs, milk and salt to a thick batter. Stir in the beans. Heat the oil to 180°C/350°F and fry the beans for 15 mins. until golden. Pile the beans onto a serving platter and garnish with parsley and lemon wedges.

GREEN BEANS WITH CHEESE BALLS

Preparation time: 55 mins.
316 calories/1323 joules

Metric/Imperial	American
750g/1½ lbs French beans, salt	1½ lbs green beans, salt
25g/1 oz butter	2 tbs butter
few sprigs parsley	few sprigs parsley
2 sprigs savory	2 sprigs savory
125g/4 oz Emmenthal cheese, grated	¼ lb Swiss cheese, grated
1 egg	1 egg
1x15ml/1 tbs flour	1 tbs flour
oil for deep frying	oil for deep frying

String and wash the beans, cut them into 3cm/1 in. lengths, and cook them in boiling, salted water for 25 mins. until tender. Melt the butter in a saucepan and toss the drained beans in it. Finely chop the parsley and savory and sprinkle them over the beans. Arrange them in a serving bowl and garnish with more parsley.
While the beans are cooking, prepare the cheese balls. Make a stiff dough with the grated cheese, egg, and flour and shape it into small balls. Deep fry them in hot oil for 10 mins. until golden. Arrange the cheese balls on top of the beans and serve immediately.

GREEN BEANS IN SOFRITO SAUCE

Preparation time: 50 mins.
77 calories/322 joules.

Metric/Imperial	American
1 slice bacon	1 slice bacon
1 thin slice ham	1 thin slice ham
1 onion	1 onion
½ green pepper, diced	½ green pepper, diced
2 tomatoes, skinned and diced	2 tomatoes, skinned and diced
1 pinch of garlic salt	1 pinch of garlic salt
175ml/6 fl oz water	¾ cup water
500g/1 lb French beans	1 lb green beans
1x15ml/1 tbs olives, chopped	1 tbs olives, chopped
2½ml/½ tsp capers, chopped	½ tsp capers, chopped
2½ml/½ tsp oregano	½ tsp oregano
1x5ml/1 tsp salt	1 tsp salt
large pinch of pepper	large pinch of pepper

The Sofrito sauce originates from the Caribbean island of Puerto Rico, where it is used in all sorts of different dishes. Vegetables, in particular, are often cooked in it.

Dice the bacon, ham, and onion and fry them in a casserole dish until the bacon is crisp and brown. Add the diced pepper and tomatoes and season with garlic salt. Pour in 125ml/4 fl oz/½ cup of water, and simmer gently for 5 mins. stirring continuously. Add the cut beans, olives, capers, oregano, salt, and pepper. Pour in 60ml/2 fl oz/ ¼ cup of water, cover, and simmer for 25 mins. until the vegetables are tender.

Top left: Green beans in batter.
Top right: Green beans with cheese balls.
Bottom: Green beans with Sofrito sauce.

Neapolitan courgettes.

NEAPOLITAN COURGETTES

Metric/Imperial

4 large courgettes
For the stuffing:
2 small onions
2x15ml/3 tbs olive oil
250g/8 oz minced beef
few sprigs parsley
150g/5 oz diced ham
1 egg
25g/1 oz Parmeasan cheese, grated
salt, white pepper
2½ml/½ tsp dried chervil
In addition:
4x15ml/4 tbs tomato ketchup
125ml/4 fl oz single cream
1 dash of Tabasco sauce
50g/2 oz butter

American

4 large zucchini

2 small onions
3 tbs olive oil

½ lb lean ground beef
few sprigs parsley
5 oz diced ham
1 egg
2 tbs Parmesan cheese, grated
salt, white pepper
½ tsp dried chervil

4 tbs tomato catsup
½ cup light cream
1 dash of Tabasco sauce
¼ cup butter

Preparation time: 1 hr.
About 660 calories/2764 joules

Preheat oven to 200°C/400°F/Gas 6.
Slice the courgettes in half lengthwise and cut off the stalk ends. Place cut side down in a pan of boiling, salted water and cook covered for 10 mins. Drain the courgettes and, with a teaspoon, scoop out most of the flesh from the centres. Dice the flesh and place it in a bowl.
For the stuffing, finely chop the onions. Heat the oil in a saucepan and fry the onions gently for 2 mins., until golden. Add the minced beef and fry for a further 5 mins. stirring frequently. Finely chop the parsley and add it to the diced courgette flesh together with the diced ham, beaten egg, Parmesan cheese, and minced beef. Season well with salt, pepper, and chervil and mix well. Spoon the stuffing into the courgette shells and place them in a greased ovenproof dish.
Mix the tomato ketchup with the cream and Tabasco sauce. Pour over the stuffed courgettes and dot with butter. Cook in the preheated oven on the centre shelf for 20 mins.

NEUCHÂTEL FONDUE

Preparation time: 30 mins.
About 990 calories/4144 joules

Metric/Imperial

1 clove garlic
250ml/8 fl oz Moselle
   or Rhine wine
1x5ml/1 tsp lemon
   juice
250g/8 oz Emmenthal
   cheese, grated
250g/8 oz Gruyére
   cheese, grated
2x5ml/2 tsp cornflour
2x15ml/2 tbs kirsch
freshly ground black
   pepper
large pinch of
   grated nutmeg
French bread to
   serve

American

1 clove garlic
1 cup Moselle or
   Rhine wine
1 tsp lemon juice
½ lb Swiss cheese,
   cheese, grated
½ lb Gruyére cheese,
   grated
2 tsp cornstarch
2 tbs kirsch
freshly ground black
   pepper
large pinch of
   grated nutmeg
French bread sticks
   to serve

A delicious, fruity white wine is produced in the Swiss canton of Neuchâtel or Neuenburg and ideally this fondue should be prepared with that wine. However, the Neuchâtel wine is rarely exported, and therefore, a good Moselle or Rhine wine has to be substituted here.

Peel and halve the garlic clove and rub it all over the inside of a fondue pan. Pour in the white wine and lemon juice and heat on the stove. Add the cheeses and stir gently until they are melted. Mix the cornflour with the kirsch and stir it into the cheese mixture. Bring to the boil and season with pepper and nutmeg. Place on the fondue burner and simmer gently.

Cut the bread into small cubes and serve separately with the cheese fondue.

To eat: spear a cube of bread with a fondue fork and dip it into the hot cheese mixture. Twist the fork a few times to prevent the cheese from running off the bread and eat it.

TIP

For a change, mix smaller amounts of different Swiss cheeses together.

Neuchâtel fondue.

MUSHROOM AND BEEF FONDUE

Preparation time: 45 mins.
About 780 calories/3265 joules

Metric/Imperial	American
For the sauces:	
250ml/8 fl oz mayonnaise	**1¼ cups mayonnaise**
2x15ml/2 tbs barbecue sauce	**2 tbs barbecue sauce**
1x5ml/1 tsp paprika pepper	**1 tsp paprika pepper**
1x5ml/1 tsp Worcester sauce	**1 tsp Worcester sauce**
dash of Tabasco sauce	**dash of Tabasco sauce**
½ banana	**½ banana**
1x15ml/1 tbs single cream	**1 tbs light cream**
1x15ml/1 tbs curry powder	**1 tbs curry powder**
1 hardboiled egg	**1 hardboiled egg**
1x5ml/1 tsp capers	**1 tsp capers**
1 shallot	**1 shallot**
1 small pickled gherkin	**1 small dill pickle**
1x15ml/1 tbs chopped parsley	**1 tbs chopped parsley**
1x5ml/1 tsp dried dill	**1 tsp dried dill**
2x15ml/2 tbs cream	**2 tbs cream**
1x15ml/1 tbs horseradish	**1 tbs horseradish**
salt, white pepper	**salt, white pepper**
sugar, a little milk if necessary	**sugar, a little milk if necessary**
For the fondue:	
500g/1 lb fillet of beef	**1 lb fillet of beef**
500g/1 lb button mushrooms	**1 lb mushrooms**
oil for deep frying	**oil for deep frying**
For the batter:	
125g/4 oz flour	**1 cup flour**
1 egg, salt	**1 egg, salt**
125ml/4 fl oz water	**½ cup water**
pinch of paprika pepper	**pinch of paprika pepper**

Like with any meat fondue the mushroom fondue, too, relies very much on the quality of the accompanying sauces. That's why we like to recommend these sauces as they bring out the delicate flavour of the mushrooms particularly well and compliment the beef as well. Start by preparing the sauces first.

Divide the mayonnaise between four small bowls.

First bowl: Mix the mayonnaise with the barbecue sauce, paprika, Worcester sauce and Tabasco and season well with salt, pepper and a pinch of sugar.

Second bowl: Mix the mayonnaise with the mashed banana, single cream and curry powder. Season with salt, pepper and sugar.

Third bowl: Finely chop the egg, capers and shallot and finely dice the pickled gherkin. Mix with the mayonnaise, parsley and dill and season with salt, pepper and sugar.

Fourth bowl: Mix the mayonnaise with the cream until smooth and stir in the grated horseradish. Season with salt, pepper and sugar.

You can thin down each sauce with a little milk if you prefer. Chill the sauces until serving.

20 minutes before eating time cut the beef fillet into cubes. Wipe and trim the mushrooms. Divide both between four plates.

Make a batter from the flour, egg, salt, water and paprika pepper and divide between four small bowls. Lay the table placing the fondue burner in the centre and surrounding it with the bowls of sauces, meat and mushroom plates and batter bowls. First heat the oil in the fondue pot on the cooker and then transfer the pot to the burner. To eat the fondue first spear a piece of meat and then a mushroom dipped in batter on the fondue fork and fry in the hot oil until done to your liking. Eat with the accompanying sauces.

You could add bottled sauces and chutneys to the fondue table.

FONDUE DIPS

Picture on pages 78/79: Chrysanthemum fire pot.

Here are a few suggestions for sauces to serve with fish or meat fondues:

Paprika dip:
mix 125g/4 oz/½ cup mayonnaise with 1x15ml/1 tbs paprika, salt, pinch of sugar, black pepper, and 2x15ml/2 tbs finely chopped tinned pimentos.

Avocado dip:
mash the flesh of 2 avocado pears and mix it with 2x15ml/2 tbs mayonnaise, juice of ½ lemon, garlic salt, white pepper, and 2x5ml/2 tsp mustard. Season well.

Mushroom dip:
drain a tin of mushrooms and finely chop them. Season with 2x5ml/2 tsp lemon juice and 5 dashes of Tabasco sauce. Stir in 125g/4 oz/½ cup mayonnaise, and season well with salt, sugar, and white pepper.

Cream dip:
whip 125ml/4 fl oz/½ cup whipping cream until stiff and season with 2x5ml/2 tsp lemon juice, 1x5ml/ 1 tsp mustard, pinch of sugar, salt, and white pepper. Stir in 2x15ml/2 tbs snipped chives and 1x15ml/1 tbs tomato ketchup.

Oil and vinegar dip:
mix 4x15ml/4 tbs oil with 2x15ml/2 tbs lemon vinegar, 1x5ml/1 tsp mustard, and 1 finely chopped onion. Add 2x15ml/2 tbs grated horseradish, a pinch of sugar, salt, and pepper. Sir in 2x15ml/2 tbs chopped parsley and leave to marinade for 1 hr. Taste for seasoning.

CHRYSANTHEMUM FIRE POT

Chu-bua-buo

Preparation time: 45 mins. plus as long as you need to enjoy the feast
About 310 calories/1297 joules

Metric/Imperial	American
250g/8 oz pork fillet	½ lb pork fillet
250g/8 oz fillet of beef	½ lb fillet of beef
175g/6 oz chicken breast, skinned and boned	6 oz chicken breast, skinned and boned
250g/8 oz calves liver	½ lb calves liver
250g/8 oz fillet of sole	½ lb fillet of sole
125g/4 oz Chinese noodles	¼ lb Chinese noodles
500ml/16 fl oz warm water	2 cups warm water
250g/8 oz large prawns	½ lb large shrimps or crayfish
500g/1 lb celery	1 lb celery
250g/8 oz fresh spinach	½ lb fresh spinach
For the sauce:	
60ml/2 fl oz soya sauce	¼ cup soya sauce
2x15ml/2 tbs sesame or vegetable oil	2 tbs sesame or vegetable oil
2x15ml/2 tbs rice wine or dry sherry	2 tbs rice wine or dry sherry
3 eggs	3 eggs
2 litres/3½ pints chicken stock	9 cups chicken stock

All fire pot dishes come from China as only there can you get the traditional fire pot. This is a table-top burner with a built-in charcoal chimney in the centre. A large ovenproof glass bowl or fondue pot makes a good substitute if set over a burner.

Pat the meats, liver, and sole fillets dry on kitchen paper and place them in the freezer for 30 mins. to make them easier to slice very thinly. Slice them all in strips about 2½cm/1 in.x5cm/2 in. long. Soak the Chinese noodles for 30 mins. in warm water and then drain. Cut them into 10cm/4 in. lengths. Shell the prawns. Wash and trim the celery and cut it into strips. Blanch it in boiling water for 4 mins., drain, and pat dry. Wash and trim the spinach and pat dry.

Place the meats, fish, prawns, noodles, and vegetables in small bowls and put them on a large table. For the sauce, mix the soya sauce with the oil, rice wine or sherry, and the beaten eggs. Divide the sauce between 6 small bowls, and arrange 1 each with a fondue fork and a second small bowl at each place.

Heat the chicken stock and pour it into the fondue pot or ovenproof glass dish. Place this over a burner in the middle of the table. Each guest spears a piece of meat on to a fork. Then the meat is cooked in the hot stock until tender, and dipped into a bowl of sauce before being eaten. All the meat and fish are eaten first to flavour the broth. The noodles and vegetables are then cooked in the broth for 1 min., and are served to each person as a delicious soup afterwards.

FONDUE FOR CHILDREN AND ADULTS

Preparation time: 40 mins.
About 875 calories/3662 joules

Metric/Imperial	American
For dipping:	
2 bananas	2 bananas
juice ½ lemon	juice ½ lemon
1 small tin pine-apple cubes	1 small can pine-apple cubes
1 small jar cocktail cherries	1 small jar cocktail cherries
1 small tin sliced peaches	1 small can sliced peaches
1 small tin mandarin oranges	1 small tin mandarin oranges
For the fondue mixture:	
200g/6 oz plain chocolate	6 oz plain chocolate
125ml/4 fl oz milk	½ cup milk
50g/2 oz chopped almonds	½ cup chopped almonds
3x15ml/3 tbs honey	3 tbs honey
3x15ml/3 tbs cocoa powder	3 tbs cocoa powder
1 pinch of salt	1 pinch of salt
2x15ml/2 tbs caster sugar	2 tbs granulated sugar

Fondue for children: a super idea for the next birthday party. And for adults, it makes an original dessert.

First prepare the ingredients for dipping. Slice the bananas and sprinkle them with lemon juice. Drain the pineapple, cocktail cherries, peaches, and mandarin oranges. Arrange the fruit attractively in small bowls.

For the fondue mixture, melt the chocolate over a pan of hot water and beat in the milk. Continue cooking on top of the stove. Add the almonds, honey, cocoa, salt, and sugar. As soon as the mixture comes to the boil, remove from the stove and place over a burner to keep warm.

To eat: spear a piece of fruit on to a fondue fork or wooden skewer and dip it into the chocolate mixture.

Serve with wafer biscuits, sponge fingers, or any other plain biscuits.

Fondue for children and adults.

COFFEE CREAM

Preparation time without chilling: 30 mins.
About 370 calories/1549 joules

Metric/Imperial	American
500ml/16 fl oz milk	2 cups milk
1 pinch of salt	1 pinch of salt
1 small piece of vanilla pod	1 small piece of vanilla pod
25g/1 oz instant coffee powder	2 tbs instant coffee powder
125g/4 oz icing sugar	¾ cup confectioners' sugar
2 eggs, 3 egg yolks	2 eggs, 3 egg yolks
butter for greasing	butter for greasing
For the decoration:	
125ml/4 fl oz whipping cream	½ cup whipping cream
2x15ml/2 tbs caster sugar	2 tbs granulated sugar
2½ml/½ tsp vanilla essence	½ tsp vanilla flavoring
25g/1 oz plain chocolate, grated	1 oz plain chocolate, grated

Preheat oven to 200°C/400°F/Gas 6.

Bring the milk with the salt, split vanilla pod, instant coffee, and icing sugar to the boil, and then cool slightly. Beat the eggs with the egg yolks in a bowl and carefully whisk in the cooled milk mixture. Grease four ramekin dishes with butter and fill them with the coffee mixture. Place them in a roasting tin half filled with water, cover, and cook in the preheated oven on the centre shelf for 20 mins.

Remove the ramekins from the oven and leave to cool. Cover, and chill in the refrigerator until just before serving. Whip cream with the sugar and

Coffee cream.

vanilla essence until stiff. Invert the coffee creams on to individual dessert plates. Spoon the cream into a piping bag and pipe swirls around the creams. Decorate with grated chocolate.

TIP

With 250ml/8 fl oz/1 cup of leftover coffee, you can easily prepare a simple coffee cream: stir in 75g/3 oz caster sugar, 2x15ml/2 tbs cognac, and 2x15ml/2 tbs gelatine. Before setting, fold in 250ml/8 fl oz/1 cup whipped cream.

AMBROSIA

Preparation time: 45 mins.
510 calories/2134 joules

Metric/Imperial	American
500ml/16 fl oz soured cream	2 cups sour cream
200g/6 oz caster sugar	¾ cup granulated sugar
1x15ml/1 tbs brandy	1 tbs brandy
2½ml/½ tsp vanilla essence	½ tsp vanilla flavoring
15g/½ oz gelatine	½ oz gelatine
few drops red food colouring (optional)	few drops red food coloring (optional)
375g/12 oz tinned cherries, stoned	12 oz canned cherries, stoned
250ml/8 fl oz whipping cream	1 cup whipping cream

Beat the soured cream until fluffy and stir in the sugar, brandy, and vanilla. Soak the gelatine in a little water and dissolve it over a pan of hot water. Cool and stir well into the soured cream mixture. Add red food colouring if desired. Drain the cherries. Whip the cream until stiff. Fill 4 serving glasses with alternate layers of soured cream mixture, cherries, and whipped cream. Garnish with a swirl of whipped cream and a cherry.

Ambrosia.

STRAWBERRIES SAN REMO

Preparation time: 35 mins.
About 285 calories/1193 joules

Metric/Imperial	American
250g/8 oz strawberries	½ lb strawberries
3x15ml/3 tbs caster sugar	3 tbs granulated sugar
For the cream:	
3 egg yolks	3 egg yolks
6x15ml/6 tbs caster sugar	6 tbs granulated sugar
2½ml/½ tsp vanilla essence	½ tsp vanilla flavoring
pinch of nutmeg	pinch of nutmeg
3x5ml/3 tsp cognac	3 tsp cognac
250ml/8 fl oz whipping cream	1 cup whipping cream
For the decoration:	
25g/1 oz plain chocolate, grated	1 oz plain chocolate, grated
1x15ml/1 tbs flaked almonds	1 tbs flaked almonds

Hull the strawberries and cut them in half. Sprinkle with sugar, cover, and set aside for 15 mins.
For the cream, beat the egg yolks with the sugar, vanilla, nutmeg, and cognac until light and fluffy. Whip the cream and fold into the egg mixture. Divide the strawberries between 4 glass dishes or glasses and pour the cream over. Chill in the refrigerator for 10 mins. Decorate with grated chocolate and flaked almonds.

Above: Strawberry San Remo.
Below: Blackberry cream.

FIGS IN PORT

Preparation time: 25 mins.
About 405 calories/1695 joules

Metric/Imperial	American
For the syrup:	
250g/8 oz caster sugar	1 cup granulated sugar
250ml/8 fl oz water	1 cup water
250ml/8 fl oz port	1 cup port
500g/1 lb fresh figs	1 lb fresh figs

For the syrup, mix the sugar with the water and bring to the boil. Stir until the sugar is dissolved. Pour in the port. Add the whole figs and cook for about 10 mins. Leave to cool, and chill in the refrigerator until serving.

HONEY YOGURT

Preparation time: 15 mins.
About 265 calories/1109 joules

Metric/Imperial	American
4x150 ml/4x5 oz cartons natural yogurt	4x5 oz cartons natural yogurt
3 oranges	3 oranges
1 lemon	1 lemon
40g/1½ oz caster sugar	3 tbs granulated sugar
3 egg yolks	3 egg yolks
2x15ml/2 tbs honey	2 tbs honey

Place the yogurt in a bowl. Squeeze the juice from 2 of the oranges and the lemon and beat it into the yogurt. Stir in the sugar, egg yolks, and honey. Divide the mixture between 4 glass bowls. Peel the remaining orange, cut it into 4 slices, and place 1 on each yogurt.

BLACKBERRY CREAM

Preparation time: 30 mins.
477 calories/1996 joules

Metric/Imperial	American
500g/1 lb blackberries	1 lb blackberries
125g/4 oz quark or low fat soft cheese	¼ lb quark or low fat soft cheese
1x150ml/5 oz carton of natural yogurt	1x5 oz carton of natural yogurt
4x15ml/4 tbs honey	4 tbs honey
2 eggs	2 eggs
1 glass aquavit or vodka	1 glass aquavit or vodka
juice 1 lemon	juice 1 lemon
125ml/4 fl oz whipping cream	½ cup whipping cream
16 small almond macaroons	16 small almond macaroons
16 walnut halves	16 walnut halves

This rich and tasty dessert comes from Sweden. Sieve the blackberries into a bowl, reserving a few for decoration. Separate the eggs. Add the cheese, yogurt, honey, egg yolks, aquavit or vodka, and lemon juice to the blackberries and beat until light and creamy. Separately whip the egg whites and the whipping cream until stiff and fold both gently into the blackberry mixture. Divide it between 4 glass bowls and chill in the refrigerator. Just before serving, decorate the dessert with the macaroons, reserved blackberries, and walnut halves.

RASPBERRY DESSERT

Preparation time: 25 mins.
About 520 calories/2176 joules

Metric/Imperial	American
500g/1 lb fresh or frozen raspberries	1 lb fresh or frozen raspberries
250g/8 oz icing sugar	1½ cups confectioners' sugar
1 egg white	1 egg white
juice ½ lemon	juice ½ lemon
4x15ml/4 tbs raspberry liqueur	4 tbs raspberry liqueur
125ml/4 fl oz whipping cream	½ cup whipping cream
8 wafer biscuits	8 wafer biscuits

Hull and pick over the raspberries. (Defrost frozen berries.)
Reserve a few for decoration, and crush the remaining raspberries with a fork. Stir in the sifted icing sugar.
Whip the egg white until stiff and fold into the raspberries. Stir in the lemon juice and raspberry liqueur. Whip the cream and gently fold into the mixture. Divide the mixture between 4 glasses and decorate with the reserved raspberries and the wafers.

Raspberry dessert.

Redcurrant jelly dish.

BILBERRY STRUDEL

Preparation time: 1¼ hrs.
About 615 calories/2574 joules

Metric/Imperial	American
250g/8 oz frozen puff pastry	½ lb frozen puff paste
250g/8 oz fresh or frozen bilberries	½ lb fresh or frozen blueberries
50g/2 oz caster sugar	¼ cup granulated sugar
1 egg	1 egg
50g/2 oz ground hazelnuts	½ cup ground hazelnuts
1x5ml/1 tsp cinnamon	1 tsp cinnamon

Preheat oven to 200°C/400°F/Gas 6.
Defrost the puff pastry according to instructions on the packet. Pick over fresh bilberries, defrost frozen ones. Sprinkle them with sugar.
Roll out the pastry thinly to a large rectangle. Separate the egg and brush the pastry with lightly beaten egg white. Sprinkle over the ground hazelnuts and cinnamon, leaving a 2½cm/1 in. border all round. Finally, spread over the sugared bilberries. Loosely roll up the strudel and press the edges together firmly. Carefully place it on a dampened baking sheet and brush it with beaten egg yolk. Bake in the preheated oven on the centre shelf for 35 mins.

REDCURRANT JELLY DISH

Preparation time without chilling: 40 mins.
About 820 calories/3432 joules

Metric/Imperial	American
For the jelly:	
1kg/2¼ lbs redcurrants	2¼ lbs redcurrants
400g/14 oz caster sugar	1¾ cups granulated sugar
500ml/16 fl oz water	2 cup water
2½ml/½ tsp vanilla essence	¼ tsp vanilla flavoring
½ cinnamon stick	½ cinnamon stick
40g/1½ oz gelatine	1½ oz gelatine
For the decoration:	
250ml/8 fl oz whipping cream	1 cup whipping cream
2x15ml/2 tbs caster sugar	2 tbs granulated sugar
few drops vanilla essence	few drops vanilla flavoring
75g/3 oz flaked almonds	½ cup flaked almonds

With a fork, strip the redcurrants from the stalks and place them in a bowl. Sprinkle them with sugar and leave them to draw juice for about 2 hrs. Drain, catching the juice in a saucepan. Mix the water with the juice, add the vanilla essence and cinnamon stick, and bring to the boil. Meanwhile, soak the gelatine in a little water. Stir the redcurrants into the boiling juice, return to the boil, and remove from the heat. Stir in the gelatine, making sure that it is completely dissolved. Leave to cool, stirring occasionally to disperse the fruit evenly. When the jelly starts to set, pour it into a rinsed ring mould. Place it in the refrigerator to set for at least 1 hr.
For the decoration, whip the cream with the sugar and vanilla until stiff and spoon it into a piping bag. Invert the redcurrant jelly on to a serving plate and surround it with swirls of whipped cream. Sprinkle the flaked almonds over the cream and serve chilled.

Bilberry strudel is filled with a mixture of bilberries, hazelnuts, and cinnamon.

Tutti frutti:
a delicious concoction of mixed fruit,
cream, and eggs topped with meringue.

TUTTI FRUTTI

Serves 8.

Preparation time: 1½ hrs.
About 435 calories/1821 joules

Metric/Imperial

100g/4 oz fresh or
  frozen strawberries
100g/4 oz fresh or
  frozen raspberries
4 tinned peach
  halves
4 tinned pear halves
100g/4 oz cherries
5x15ml/5 tbs rum
For the cream:
500ml/16 fl oz whip-
  ping cream
grated rind 1 lemon
75g/3 oz cornflour
6 egg yolks
75g/3 oz caster
  sugar
For the meringue:
6 egg whites
25g/1 oz caster
  sugar

American

¼ lb fresh or frozen
  strawberries
¼ lb fresh or frozen
  raspberries
4 canned peach
  halves
4 canned pear halves
¼ lb cherries
5 tbs rum

2 cups whipping
  cream
grated rind 1 lemon
¾ cup cornstarch
6 egg yolks
⅓ cup granulated
  sugar

6 egg whites
2 tbs granulated
  sugar

Tutti frutti is Italian for 'all fruit'. All kinds of fruit can be used for this dessert: fresh, frozen, tinned, or poached in syrup. In summer, you could make use of the abundance of fresh fruit available, layering it with a sprinkling of sugar. In winter use tinned or forzen fruit. This recipe uses a mixture of all kinds.

Hull the strawberries and raspberries or defrost frozen berries. Drain the peaches and pears, and cut them into cubes. Stone the cherries. Layer the fruit in a ovenproof glass dish and sprinkle each layer with rum. Cover and set aside.

For the cream, whip the whipping cream until it just holds its shape and mix it with the lemon rind, cornflour, egg yolks, and sugar. Over a pan of boiling water, whisk the mixture to a thick cream. Remove from the heat and continue whisking until it is cold. Pour it over the fruit. Whip the egg whites to a stiff snow and fold in the sugar. Spread the meringue mixture over the cream and brown it under a hot grill. Remove and serve.

Cherries jubilee.

Parisian baked apples are prepared with mixed fruit and calvados.

PARISIAN BAKED APPLES

Preparation time: 50 mins.
469 calories/1963 joules

Metric/Imperial	American
1 small tin apricots	1 small can apricots
1x5ml/1 tsp cornflour	1 tsp cornstarch
4 cooking apples	4 cooking apples
1 small tin pears	1 small can pears
1 small tin cherries	1 small can cherries
25g/1 oz butter	2 tbs butter
1 small tin pine-apple cubes	1 small can pine-apple cubes
2x15ml/2 tbs caster sugar	2 tbs granulated sugar
2x15ml/2 tbs flaked almonds	2 tbs flaked almonds
4x5ml/4 tsp calvados	4 tsp calvados

Preheat oven to 220°C/425°F/Gas 7.
Sieve the apricots into a saucepan and bring them to the boil. Mix the cornflour with a little water and thicken the apricot purée, with it. Cool, stirring occasionally. Core the apples, dice the pears, and stone the cherries. Melt the butter, and add the pineapple, pears, cherries, sugar, and almonds. Stir in the apricot purée. Fill the apples with the fruit mixture. Keep any remaining mixture warm. Bake the apples in the preheated oven on the centre shelf for 25 mins.
Divide the remaining fruit mixture between 4 dessert plates and place the baked apples on top. Pour 1x5ml/1 tsp calvados over each and serve immediately.

CHERRIES JUBILEE

Preparation time: 15 mins.
About 270 calories/1130 joules

Metric/Imperial	American
3x15ml/3 tbs red-currant jelly	3 tbs redcurrant jelly
1x15ml/1 tbs butter	1 tbs butter
2 cups preserved black cherries	2 cups preserved black cherries
125ml/4 fl oz kirsch or 2 tbs each of brandy and cherry brandy	½ cup kirsch or 2 tbs each of brandy and cherry brandy
500ml/16 fl oz vanilla ice cream	2 cups vanilla ice cream

In the USA, this dish has become a favourite dessert, and it is usually served on special occasions.
Melt the redcurrant jelly in an ovenproof dish or frying pan and stir in the butter until it dissolves. Add the cherries and heat through. Pour the kirsch or brandies into a large metal ladle and hold it over a naked flame to heat the alcohol. Pour over the cherries and set alight. Divide the ice cream between 4 dessert dishes. As soon as the flames die down, spoon the hot cherries over the ice cream and serve immediately.

MENU

CHICORY AND PRAWN BOATS
ROAST BEEF WITH ORANGES
PEACH MELBA

CHICORY AND PRAWN BOATS

Preparation time: 25 mins.
208 calories/870 joules

Metric/Imperial	American
2 heads of chicory	2 heads of Belgian endive
250g/8 oz prawns	½ lb shrimps
For the dressing:	
100g/4 oz mayonnaise	½ cup mayonnaise
1x5ml/1 tsp lemon juice	1 tsp lemon juice
2x15ml/2 tbs single cream	2 tbs light cream
salt, pepper	salt, pepper
1 pinch of sugar	1 pinch of sugar
1x15ml/1 tbs paprika	1 tbs paprika
2 stuffed olives	2 stuffed olives
1 sprig dill	1 sprig dill

Cut off the root ends of the chicory and separate the heads into leaves. Divide the prawns between the leaves. For the dressing, mix the mayonnaise with the lemon juice and cream and season with salt, pepper, sugar, and paprika. Pour the dressing over the prawns. Garnish the chicory boats with sliced olives and dill.

Serve with brown bread and butter as a starter or light snack.

Chicory and prawn boats.

ROAST BEEF WITH ORANGES

Preparation time: 1 hr. 5 mins.
About 840 calories/3516 joules

Metric/Imperial	American
1kg/2¼ lbs topside of beef	2¼ lbs round of beef
salt, freshly ground black pepper	salt, freshly ground black pepper
1 large pinch of dried thyme	1 large pinch of dried thyme
5x15ml/5 tbs oil	5 tbs oil
juice 2 oranges	juice 2 oranges
For the sauce:	
125ml/4 fl oz hot beef stock	½ cup hot beef stock
1x15ml/1 tbs corn-flour	1 tbs cornstarch
125ml/4 fl oz single cream	½ cup light cream
2½ml/½ tsp grated orange rind	½ tsp grated orange rind
salt, pepper	salt, pepper
pinch of sugar	pinch of sugar
For the garnish:	
1 orange	1 orange
2 tbs each of Grand Marnier and brandy	2 tbs each of Grand Marnier and brandy

Preheat oven to 250°C/475°F/Gas 9.

Rinse the beef briefly under cold water and pat dry. Score the fat lightly with the point of a knife. Rub the meat all over with a mixture of salt, pepper, and thyme.

Heat the oil in an ovenproof casserole dish and fry the beef for about 10 mins. until well browned on all sides. Pour in the orange juice and cook the beef, with the fat uppermost, in the preheated oven for 30 mins. Baste the meat frequently with the juice during cooking.

Place the cooked beef on a heated serving dish, cover, and keep warm. Bring the juices and the hot stock to the boil. Pour through a sieve into a saucepan, skimming off as much fat as possible. Mix the cornflour with the cream and stir it into the sauce. Bring to the boil. Season well with grated orange rind, salt, pepper, and sugar.

Thinly slice the unpeeled orange and surround the roast beef with it. Warm the Grand Marnier and brandy in a metal ladle and pour it over the meat. Ignite, and bring to the table flaming. Serve the sauce separately.

Roast beef with oranges.

PEACH MELBA

Preparation time: 20 mins.
About 340 calories/1423 joules

Metric/Imperial

For the sauce:
250g/8 oz raspberries
6x15ml/6 tbs luke-
  warm water
125g/4 oz icing sugar
  sugar
juice ½ lemon
2x15ml/2 tbs vanilla
  sugar
2x15ml/2 tbs rasp-
  berry liqueur

In addition:
2 fresh peaches or
  4 tinned peach
  halves
250ml/8 fl oz vanilla
  ice cream

American

½ lb raspberries
6 tbs lukewarm
  water
¾ cup confectioners'
  sugar
juice ½ lemon
2 tbs vanilla flavored
  sugar
2 tbs raspberry
  liqueur

2 fresh peaches or
  4 canned peach
  halves
1 cup vanilla
  ice cream

This delicious dessert was created by Auguste Escoffier for the soprano Helen Porter Mitchell from Melbourne. Taking the name from that town, the opera singer called herself Nellie Melba.

For the sauce, purée the raspberries with the water in a blender and add the sifted icing sugar, lemon juice, vanilla sugar and raspberry liqueur. Strain and chill in the refrigerator.

Skin, halve, and stone the fresh peaches, or drain the tinned halves. With an ice cream scoop, divide the ice cream between 4 shallow dessert glasses. Top each with 1 peach half and pour over the melba sauce. Serve immediately.

MENU

SEAFOOD COCKTAIL

VEAL CORDON BLEU

RED BERRY COMPÔTE

SEAFOOD COCKTAIL

Preparation time: 25 mins.
About 290 calories/1214 joules

Metric/Imperial	American
1 grapefruit	1 grapefruit
75g/3 oz tinned mushrooms	3 oz canned mushrooms
75g/3 oz prawns	3 oz shrimps
75g/3 oz tinned lobster meat	3 oz canned lobster meat
juice ½ lemon	juice ½ lemon
salt, white pepper	salt, white pepper
For the sauce:	
50g/2 oz mayonnaise	¼ cup mayonnaise
7½ml/½ tbs tomato ketchup	½ tbs tomato catsup
2½ml/½ tsp mustard	½ tsp mustard
2½ml/½ tsp grated horseradish	½ tsp grated horseradish
1x5ml/1 tsp sherry	1 tsp sherry
1 dash of Tabasco sauce	1 dash of Tabasco sauce
1x15ml/1 tbs single cream	1 tbs light cream
For the garnish:	
8 lettuce leaves	8 lettuce leaves
12 crayfish or large prawns	12 crayfish or large shrimps
2 sprigs dill	2 sprigs dill

Peel the grapefruit and separate it into segments. Discard all the white pith. Cut each segment in half and mix with the drained and sliced mushrooms, the prawns, and the diced lobster meat. Season with lemon juice, salt and pepper. Cover and chill in the refrigerator for 15 mins. For the sauce, mix the mayonnaise with the tomato ketchup, mustard, horseradish, sherry, and tabasco. Taste for seasoning and fold in the cream.
Shred the lettuce leaves and divide them between 4 chilled glass dishes. Cover with the seafood mixture and pour the sauce over. Garnish with the crayfish or prawns and dill.

VEAL CORDON BLEU

Preparation time: 35 mins.
650 calories/2720 joules

Metric/Imperial	American
4 veal steaks, each 200g/6 oz and 2cm/¾ in. thick	4 veal steaks, each 6 oz and ¾ in. thick
salt, white pepper	salt, white pepper
4 slices ham	4 slices ham
4 slice Swiss cheese	4 slices Swiss cheese
2x15ml/2 tbs flour	2 tbs flour
2 eggs	2 eggs
3x15ml/3 tbs dried breadcrumbs	3 tbs dried breadcrumbs
40g/1½ oz butter	3 tbs butter
For the garnish:	
1 lemon	1 lemon
lettuce leaves	lettuce leaves

Veal stuffed with ham and cheese is a culinary speciality that is said to have been invented by a top Swiss chef.
Slit the veal steaks horizontally to make a deep pocket. Flatten the steaks slightly with the palm of your hand, and season them with salt and pepper. Slide a slice of ham and cheese into each pocket and fasten the opening with wooden cocktail sticks.
Cover the steaks first in flour, then in beaten egg, and finally in breadcrumbs. Heat the butter and fry the steaks for 6–8 mins. each side until well browned. Arrange them on a heated serving plate and garnish with lemon wedges and lettuce leaves.

Seafood cocktail.

Veal cordon bleu.

RED BERRY COMPÔTE

Preparation time: 40 mins.
About 180 calories/753 joules

Metric/Imperial	American
500g/1 lb straw- berries	1 lb strawberries
100g/4 oz redcurrants	¼ lb redcurrants
100g/4 oz raspberries	¼ lb raspberries
125ml/4 fl oz water	½ cup water
100g/4 oz caster sugar	½ cup granulated sugar
½ vanilla pod	½ vanilla pod
2x15ml/2 tbs brandy	2 tbs brandy

Carefully pick over the fruit, hull the strawberries, and strip the redcurrants from the stalks. Bring the water with the sugar to the boil. Split the vanilla pod and scrape out the seeds. A d to the syrup with the fruit. Simmer gently for 10 mins. and leave to cool. Before serving, stir in the brandy.
Serve with whipped cream and sponge fingers.

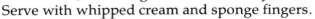

Red berry compôte.

MENU

STORCHEN COLD AVOCADO SOUP

FILLETS OF COD WITH MUSHROOM STUFFING

TIMBALE POMPADOUR

STORCHEN COLD AVOCADO SOUP

Preparation time: 25 mins.
About 365 calories/1528 joules

Metric/Imperial	American
2 medium-sized ripe avocados	2 medium-sized ripe avocados
1x5ml/1 tsp lemon juice	1 tsp lemon juice
75g/3 oz natural yogurt	⅓ cup natural yogurt
65ml/2 fl oz white wine	¼ cup white wine
250ml/8 fl oz chilled chicken stock	1 cup chilled chicken stock
175ml/6 fl oz whipping cream	¾ cup whipping cream
salt, white pepper	salt, white pepper
few dashes Worcester sauce	few dashes Worcester sauce
large pinch of grated nutmeg	large pinch of grated nutmeg

Halve the very soft avocados and remove the stones. Cut one of the avocado halves in half again crosswise and cut it into 8 thin slices. Set them aside. Skin the remaining avocados and sieve the flesh into a bowl. Sprinkle with lemon juice. Stir in the yogurt, white wine and the well chilled chicken stock. Mix well. Lightly whip the cream and fold it into the soup. Season with salt, pepper, Worcester sauce, and nutmeg. Serve garnished with the reserved avocado slices.

Serve as a starter with brown bread and butter.

FILLETS OF COD WITH MUSHROOM STUFFING

Preparation time: 1 hr.
About 410 calories/1715 joules

Metric/Imperial	American
1kg/2¼ lbs fillets of cod	2¼ lb fillets of cod
juice 1 lemon	juice 1 lemon
250g/8 oz mushrooms	½ lb mushrooms
1 small onion	1 small onion
25g/1 oz butter or margarine	2 tbs butter or margarine
2x15ml/2 tbs breadcrumbs	2 tbs breadcrumbs
2 eggs	2 eggs
margarine for greasing	margarine for greasing
salt, pepper	salt, pepper
250ml/8 fl oz soured cream	1 cup sour cream

Preheat oven to 180°C/350°F/Gas 4.

Wash and dry the fillet of cod and cut it into 4 rectangles. Sprinkle them with lemon juice. Roughly chop the mushrooms and onion. Melt the butter or margarine and fry the mushrooms and onion for about 5 mins. Add the breadcrumbs. Separate 1 egg and mix the egg white into the mixture. Place the stuffing on the cod fillets and roll them up. Secure with wooden cocktail sticks. Grease an ovenproof dish and place the fish rolls upright on the bottom. Surround with any remaining stuffing. Mix the egg yolk, egg, and soured cream and season well with salt and pepper. Pour this over the fish rolls. Cook in the preheated oven on the centre shelf for 30 mins.

Tender cod fillets with mushroom.

TIMBALE POMPADOUR

Preparation time without chilling: 1 hr. 10 mins.
About 520 calories/2177 joules

Metric/Imperial	American
For the jelly:	
40g/1½ oz gelatine	1½ oz gelatine
750ml/1½ pints cherry juice	3½ cups cherry juice
For the filling:	
500ml/1 pint milk	2 cups milk
¼ vanilla pod	¼ vanilla pod
25g/1 oz caster sugar	2 tbs granulated sugar
3 egg yolks	3 egg yolks
25g/1 oz gelatine	1 oz gelatine
125ml/4 fl oz maraschino	½ cup maraschino
100g/4 oz cocktail cherries	¼ lb cocktail cherries
250ml/8 fl oz whipping cream	1 cup whipping cream
2 egg whites	2 egg whites
For the decoration:	
125ml/4 fl oz whipping cream	½ cup whipping cream
1x15ml/1 tbs caster sugar	1 tbs granulated sugar
few drops vanilla essence	few drops vanilla flavoring
12 cocktail cherries	12 cocktail cherries

For the jelly, soak the gelatine in 125ml/4 fl oz/ ½ cup of the cherry juice for 10 mins. Dissolve it over a low heat and stir in the remaining cherry juice. Rinse a round bottomed, large bowl (2 litre/ 3½ pint 9 cups capacity) with cold water. Pour in the cherry juice. Lightly oil the outside of the a smaller bowl (1 litre/1¾ pint 4½ cup) and place it inside the large bowl. Weight the small bowl with potatoes or something similar to enable the cherry jelly to come right up the sides of the large bowl. Chill in the refrigerator for 1 hr.

Meanwhile, reserve 5x15ml/5 tbs of the milk and bring the remainder to the boil with the split vanilla pod and sugar. Discard the vanilla pod and cool the milk slightly. Gradually whisk in the egg yolks. Beat over low heat until the mixture becomes thick and creamy. Take care not to let it boil.

Soak the gelatine in the reserved milk for about 10 mins. Dissolve it over very low heat and stir into the egg mixture. Chill.

Halve the cocktail cherries. Whip the cream and egg whites separately until stiff and fold both into the cooled milk mixture with the cherries and maraschino.

Carefully remove the smaller bowl from inside the set cherry jelly and spoon the egg and cream mixture into the hollow. Smooth the top and cover with a plate or lid. Chill in the refrigerator for 2 hrs. until set.

Briefly dip the bowl in hot water and invert the timbale on to a serving plate. For the decoration, whip the cream with the sugar and vanilla essence and pipe rosettes onto the timbale. Place a cocktail cherry on top of each cream rosette and serve immediately.

An impressive dessert for a special dinner: timbale pompadour.

MENU

PAPAYA WITH HAM

PARISIAN LAMB CHOPS

MOCHA PARFAIT

PAPAYA WITH HAM

Preparation time: 15 mins.
About 180 calories/753 joules

Metric/Imperial	American
1 papaya	1 papaya
8 slices ham	8 slices ham
freshly ground black pepper	freshly ground black pepper
few sprigs parsley	few sprigs parsley

Peel the papaya and cut it in 4 pieces. Remove the stone and cut the flesh into finger-thick slices. Roll the papaya fingers in slices of ham and sprinkle them with pepper. Arrange them on a wooden board and garnish with sprigs of parsley.

PARISIAN LAMB CHOPS

Preparation time: 50 mins.
About 970 calories/4060 joules

Metric/Imperial	American
1x15ml/1 tbs butter	1 tbs butter
1x15ml/1 tbs flour	1 tbs flour
125ml/4 fl oz hot lamb or beef stock	½ cup hot lamb or beef stock
5x15ml/5 tbs milk	5 tbs milk
5x15ml/5 tbs white wine	5 tbs white wine
salt, white pepper	salt, white pepper
100g/4 oz cooked tongue, chopped	¼ lb cooked tongue, chopped
100g/4 oz mushrooms, chopped	4 oz mushrooms, chopped
1 tinned truffle	1 canned truffle
4 double lamb chops, 200g/6 oz each	4 double lamb chops, 6 oz each
freshly ground black pepper	freshly ground black pepper
2x15ml/2 tbs oil	2 tbs oil
180g/6½ oz tinned artichoke hearts	6½ oz canned artichoke hearts
200g/7 oz tinned madeira sauce	7 oz canned madeira sauce

Melt the butter in a saucepan and stir in the flour. Cook for 2 mins. Add the hot stock, milk, and white wine, season with salt and pepper, and cook for 5 mins., stirring occasionally. Add the chopped tongue and mushrooms. Drain and finely chop the truffle. Stir half of it into the sauce and heat through.

Meanwhile, score the fat of the lamb chops and season them with salt and black pepper. Brush both sides with oil. Place them under a hot grill and grill them for 8 mins. on each side.

Heat the artichoke hearts with their liquid in a saucepan. Heat the madeira sauce over a pan of hot water. Arrange the grilled lamb chops on a heated serving plate. Surround them with the drained artichoke hearts and place a spoonful of the tongue and mushroom mixture on each heart. Pour a little of the madeira sauce over the chops and serve the rest separately.

Well seasoned with plenty of pepper: papaya with ham.

Parisian lamb chops are served with stuffed artichoke hearts and madeira sauce.

MOCHA PARFAIT

Preparation time without freezing: 20 mins.
About 380 calories/1590 joules

Metric/Imperial	American
3 egg yolks	3 egg yolks
100g/4 oz caster sugar	½ cup granulated sugar
1x15ml/1 tbs instant coffee	1 tbs instant coffee
1x15ml/1 tbs warm water	1 tbs warm water
250ml/8 fl oz whipping cream	1 cup whipping cream
2½ml/½ tsp caster sugar	½ tsp granulated sugar
few drops of vanilla essence	few drops of vanilla flavoring
For the decoration:	
1x15ml/1 tbs grated chocolate	1 tbs grated chocolate
1x15ml/1 tbs flaked almonds	1 tbs flaked almonds

Beat the egg yolks with the sugar until light and fluffy. Dissolve the coffee in the warm water and stir into the egg mixture. Whip the cream until stiff and add the sugar and vanilla. Reserve about 2x15ml/2 tbs for decoration, and fold the remainder into the egg mixture. Divide the mixture between 4 glass dishes and place them in the icemaking compartment of the refrigerator or in the freezer for 3 hrs. until the parfaits are frozen.

Before serving, decorate the parfaits with swirls of whipped cream, grated chocolate, and almond flakes. Serve immediately.

An iced dessert that melts in the mouth: mocha parfait.

Ice cream gâteau.

ICE CREAM GÂTEAU

Serves 6.

Preparation time without freezing: 3¾ hrs.
About 450 calories/1883 joules

Metric/Imperial

For the base:
3 egg whites
150g/5 oz caster
  sugar
2½ml/½ tsp lemon
  juice
margarine for
  greasing
For the ice cream:
5 egg yolks
150g/5 oz caster
  sugar
6x15ml/6 tbs white
  wine
15g/½ oz gelatine
375ml/12 fl oz whip-
  ping cream
2x15ml/2 tbs cocoa
  powder
6x15ml/6 tbs fresh or
  frozen raspberries

American

3 egg whites
⅔ cup granulated
  sugar
½ tsp lemon juice

margarine for
  greasing

5 egg yolks
⅔ cup granulated
  sugar
6 tbs white
  wine
½ oz gelatine
1½ cups whipping
  cream
2 tbs cocoa powder

6 tbs fresh or
  frozen raspberries

For the decoration:
125ml/4 fl oz whip-
  ping cream
1x15ml/1 tbs caster
  sugar
few drops vanilla
  essence
100g/4 oz plain
  chocolate flakes
50g/2 oz milk
  chocolate

½ cup whipping
  cream
1 tbs granulated
  sugar
few drops vanilla
  flavoring
¼ lb plain choco-
  late flakes
2 oz milk
  chocolate

Preheat oven to 107°C/225°F/Gas ¼.

For the base, whip the egg whites to a stiff snow and gradually beat in the sugar and lemon juice. Line a baking sheet with greased aluminium foil and, using a cake tin as a guide, mark a circle on the foil. Spoon the meringue mixture into a piping bag and pipe a round base in spirals from the outside inwards. Bake in the preheated oven on the bottom shelf for about 3 hrs.

Turn off the oven and leave the meringue base in it to dry out and cool. Carefully pull off the aluminium foil from the bottom of the base and place the base inside a spring-release cake tin.

While the base is baking, prepare the ice cream. Beat the egg yolks, sugar, and white wine over a pan of hot water until the sugar has dissolved and the mixture is very pale and creamy. Soak the gelatine in a little cold water and stir it into the egg mixture. Remove from the heat and beat until the gelatine is dissolved and the mixture is quite cold. Whip the cream until stiff and fold into the mixture. Divide the mixture into 3 portions and stir the cocoa powder into the 1st portion. Spread this over the meringue base and place it in the icemaking compartment of the refrigerator for 5 mins. For the 2nd layer, rub the raspberries (thawed if frozen) through a sieve and fold into the 2nd portion of cream mixture. Spread the over the chocolate layer. Spread the remaining cream mixture over the top. Freeze the ice cream gâteau for about 7 hrs, then remove it from the tin.

For the decoration, whip the cream with the sugar and vanilla and pipe swirls on top of the gâteau. Decorate with flakes of plain chocolate and curls of milk chocolate. Serve immediately.

Iced chartreuse: an exquisite cream dessert.

ICED VANILLA MOUSSE

Preparation time without freezing: 30 mins.
About 520 calories/2176 joules

Metric/Imperial	American
2 eggs	2 eggs
75g/3 oz icing sugar	⅔ cup confectioners' sugar
2x15ml/2 tbs vanilla sugar	2 tbs vanilla flavored sugar
250ml/8 fl oz whipping cream	1 cup whipping cream
For the decoration:	
125ml/4 fl oz whipping cream	½ cup whipping cream
2x15ml/2 tbs vanilla sugar	2 tbs vanilla flavored sugar
4 chocolate flakes	4 chocolate flakes
4 cocktail cherries	4 cocktail cherries

Separate the eggs. Over bowl of hot water, beat the egg yolks with the icing and vanilla sugar until pale and creamy. Remove from the heat and leave to cool. Whip the egg whites and the cream separately to a firm snow and fold them into the egg mixture. Rinse a large ice cube tray with cold water and spread with the mousse. Freeze for about 3 hrs.

Whip the cream with the vanilla sugar and spoon it into a piping bag. Remove the ice cube tray from the freezer and dip it into hot water. Invert the iced mousse on to a plate and divide it into 4 portions. Place these on 4 individual glass dishes and decorate them with swirls of whipped cream, crumbled chocolate flakes, and cocktail cherries.

NOTE
Vary the flavourings by adding grated chocolate, instant coffee, ground nuts, glacé fruit, or liqueurs.

ICED CHARTREUSE

Preparation time: 2½ hrs.
About 905 calories/3788 joules

Metric/Imperial	American
1 litre/1¾ pints whipping cream	4½ cups whipping cream
100g/4 oz icing sugar	¾ cup confectioners' sugar
8x15ml/8 tbs green chartreuse	8 tbs green chartreuse

Whip the cream with the sieved icing sugar until stiff and fold in the chartreuse. Pour into a loaf tin, cover, and place in the deep freeze or icemaking compartment of the refrigerator for about 2 hrs.

Dip the tin briefly in hot water and invert the iced chartreuse on to a plate. With a knife dipped in warm water, cut slices and arrange them on chilled dessert plates. Serve immediately.

Iced chartreuse can be served without decoration, but it could be decorated with whipped cream and pistachio nuts.

Serve with sponge fingers or fan wafers.

NOTE
You can vary this dessert by substituting any other liqueur for chartreuse.

YOGURT ICE CREAM

Preparation time without freezing: 45 mins.
About 390 calories/1632 joules

Metric/Imperial	American
8 sponge fingers	8 sponge fingers
2x15ml/2 tbs maraschino	2 tbs maraschino
4x150g/5 oz cartons natural yogurt	4x5 oz cartons natural yogurt
200g/6 oz caster sugar	¾ cup granulated sugar
1 pinch of salt	1 pinch of salt
75g/3 oz plain chocolate	3 oz plain chocolate

Crush the sponge fingers into a bowl and sprinkle them with maraschino. Chill for 30 mins. in the refrigerator. Beat the yogurt with the sugar and salt until creamy and grate in the chocolate. Beat for a further 10 mins., then mix with the sponge mixture. Pour into a freezerproof bowl and freeze for about 4 hrs. Cut the frozen yogurt in cubes and serve on glass dishes.

Serve with hot raspberry sauce and sponge fingers.

FRUIT SORBET

Serves 6.

Preparation time without freezing: 25 mins.
About 295 calories/1234 joules

Metric/Imperial	American
750ml/27 fl oz water	3½ cups water
375g/12 oz caster sugar	1½ cups granulated sugar
4x15ml/4 tbs lemon juice	4 tbs lemon juice
500ml/16 fl oz strawberry, raspberry, redcurrant, cherry, or orange juice	2 cups strawberry, raspberry, redcurrant, cherry, or orange juice
1 egg white	1 egg white
1x15ml/1 tbs caster sugar	1 tbs granulated sugar

Fruit sorbet is always prepared from fresh fruit juice.

Slowly bring the water and sugar to the boil, stirring to dissolve the sugar. When the mixture reaches boiling point, simmer it for 5 mins. Leave to cool.

Measure out 500ml/16 fl oz/2 cups of the syrup and mix with the lemon juice and any of the other fruit juices. Pour into a bowl and freeze for 2½ hrs. Stir the mixture every 30 mins.

Chill a second bowl and 6 serving glasses.

A crowning finale to a special dinner: flaming ice cream mountain decorated with fresh strawberries.

Whip the egg white to a stiff snow and sprinkle in the sugar. Place the frozen fruit syrup mixture in the chilled bowl and quickly fold in the sweetened egg white. Divide the sorbet between the serving glasses and serve immediately.

MANGO WITH RUM

Preparation time without marinading: 15 mins.
About 340 calories/1423 joules

Metric/Imperial	American
2 mangoes	2 mangoes
4x15ml/4 tbs caster sugar	4 tbs granulated sugar
8x15ml/8 tbs rum	8 tbs rum
12 scoops of lemon sorbet	12 scoops of lemon sherbet

Peel off the tough skin of the mangoes and cut the flesh into cubes, removing the stones. Place the mango cubes in a bowl and sprinkle them with sugar and rum. Cover and leave to marinade in the refrigerator for 1 hr.

Divide the sorbet between 4 glass dishes and top with the rum- soaked mango. Serve immediately.

A dessert with a kick: mango with rum.

FLAMING ICE CREAM MOUNTAIN

Serves 6.

Preparation time without freezing: 1 hr.
About 400 calories/1674 joules

Metric/Imperial	American
For the ice cream:	
50g/2 oz plain chocolate	2 oz plain chocolate
75g/3 oz caster sugar	1/3 cup granulated sugar
125ml/4 fl oz water	1/2 cup water
4 egg yolks	4 egg yolks
1 pinch of salt	1 pinch of salt
4x15ml/4 tbs rum	4 tbs rum
250ml/8 fl oz whipping cream	1 cup whipping cream
In addition:	
1 ready-baked sponge base, 24cm/9½ in.	1 ready-baked sponge base, 9½ in.
150g/5 oz strawberry jam	5 oz strawberry jelly
For the meringue:	
6 egg whites	6 egg whites
150g/5 oz caster sugar	2/3 cup granulated sugar
1 pinch of salt	1 pinch of salt
2x15ml/2 tbs vanilla sugar	2 tbs vanilla flavored sugar

For the decoration:	
8 fresh strawberries	8 fresh strawberries
1x15ml/1 tbs rum	1 tbs rum

For the ice cream, melt the chocolate with the sugar and water over a pan of hot water until the sugar has dissolved.

Beat the egg yolks with the salt over a pan of simmering water. Whisk in first the chocolate mixture and then, gradually, half the rum. Remove from the heat as soon as the mixture thickens, and beat until it is cold. Whip the cream and fold it in.

Soak the sponge base with the remaining rum and spread with the strawberry jam. Pile the ice cream mixture in the centre of the base, leaving a 1cm/ ½ in. border all round. Freeze for about 4 hrs.

Shortly before serving, whip the egg whites to a firm snow and fold in the caster sugar, salt, and vanilla sugar. Spoon the meringue mixture into a piping bag and pipe it all over the ice cream, making the centre a little higher than the rest. Brown the meringue under a preheated grill for 5 mins.

Remove from the grill and decorate with the strawberries. Pour the rum over the meringue, ignite it, and serve still flaming. Take care not to burn the meringue as it will become bitter.

Brazilian chocolate ice cream cup.

BRAZILIAN CHOCOLATE ICE CREAM CUP

Preparation time: 25 mins.
640 calories/2679 joules

Metric/Imperial	American
1 small tin pine-apple cubes	1 small can pine-apple cubes
8x15ml/8 tbs white rum	8 tbs white rum
50g/2 oz almond slivers	½ cup almond slivers
25g/1 oz butter	2 tbs butter
chocolate ice cream	chocolate ice cream
250ml/8 fl oz whip-ping cream	1 cup whipping cream

Drain the pineapple and pour the rum over. Leave to marinade for 30 mins.

Meanwhile fry the almond slivers in the butter until golden. Cool. Layer 4 glass coupe dishes with the chocolate ice cream and drained pineapple cubes. Pour the rum marinade over. Whip the cream and pipe big swirls on top. Decorate with the almond slivers.

FRUIT WATER ICE

Preparation time without freezing: 25 mins.
About 300 calories/1255 joules

Metric/Imperial	American
500g/1 lb straw-berries, raspber-ries, apricots, blackberries or bilberries	1 lb strawberries, raspberries, apricots, black-berries or blueberries
500ml/16 fl oz water	2 cups water
250g/8 oz caster sugar	1 cup granulated sugar
juice 1 lemon	juice 1 lemon

You can make fruit water ices with any fruit, including frozen fruit in the winter.

Wash and pick over the fruit and reserve a few for decoration. Bring the water to the boil and add the fruit and sugar. Simmer for 5 mins. Press the fruit and syrup through a sieve, extracting as much of the purée as possible. Add the lemon juice and spoon the purée into ice trays. Freeze for 3 hrs.

Serve decorated with the reserved fruit.

Serve with whipped cream and sponge fingers or fan wafers.

ALSAÇE CHEESECAKE

Serves 8.

Preparation time without soaking: 1 hr. 20 mins.
About 465 calories/1946 joules

Metric/Imperial	American
For the filling:	
250ml/8 fl oz red wine	1 cup red wine
1x3cm/1 in. cinnamon stick	1x1 in. cinnamon stick
4 cloves	4 cloves
375g/12 oz stoned prunes	¾ lb stoned prunes
For the pastry:	
250g/8 oz plain flour	2 cups all purpose flour
pinch of salt	pinch of salt
150g/5 oz butter or margarine	⅔ cup butter or margarine
60g/2½ oz caster sugar	¼ cup granulated sugar
1 egg	1 egg
For the topping:	
750g/1½ lbs quark or curd cheese	1½ lbs quark or curd cheese
3 egg yolks	3 egg yolks
75g/3 oz cornflour	¾ cup cornstarch
250ml/8 fl oz whipping cream	1 cup whipping cream
75g/3 oz caster sugar	⅓ cup granulated sugar
3 egg whites	3 egg whites
2x15ml/2 tbs vanilla sugar	2 tbs vanilla flavored sugar
grated rind ½ lemon	grated rind ½ lemon
icing sugar	confectioners' sugar

Preheat oven to 200°C/400°F/Gas 6.

For the filling, bring the red wine to the boil with the cinnamon stick and cloves. Pour this over the prunes and leave them to soften overnight.

Sieve the flour and salt into a bowl. Dice the butter or margarine and rub into the flour. Add the sugar. Make a hollow in the centre, and stir in the beaten egg. Mix together with a knife, and then knead to a smooth dough with your hands. Shape into a ball, wrap in greaseproof paper and chill in the refrigerator for 30 mins.

On a floured board, roll out the pastry and line a 26cm/10 in. cake tin with removable base.

Drain the soaked prunes and discard the cinnamon stick and cloves. Cover the base of the pastry with the prunes.

Mix the quark or curd cheese with the egg yolks and cornflour. Whip the cream and sweeten with ⅔ of the sugar. In a separate bowl, beat the egg whites to a firm snow and fold in the remaining caster sugar and the vanilla sugar. Carefully fold the cream, egg whites, and lemon rind into the quark mixture and mix well. Spread the cheese mixture over the prunes and smooth the top with a wetted knife. Bake in the preheated oven on the bottom shelf for 55 mins.

Remove the cheesecake from the oven, take it out of the tin, and cool it on a wire rack. Dust with sifted icing sugar and serve cold.

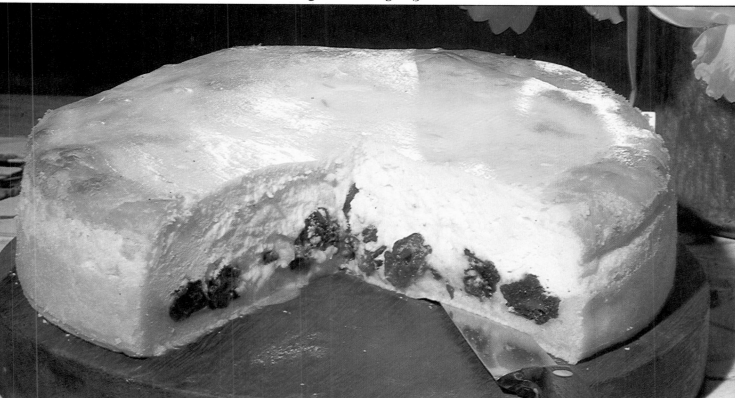

Alsaçe cheesecake.

SACHERTORTE

Serves 8.

Preparation time: 2 hrs. 20 mins.
About 520 calories/2176 joules

Metric/Imperial	American
250g/8 oz plain chocolate	½ lb plain chocolate
200g/6 oz butter	¾ cup butter
200g/6 oz caster sugar	¾ cup granulated sugar
pinch of salt	pinch of salt
8 eggs, separated	8 eggs, separated
2½ml/½ tsp vanilla essence	½ tsp vanilla flavoring
250g/8 oz plain flour	2 cups all purpose flour
margarine for greasing	margarine for greasing
4x15ml/4 tbs apricot jam	4 tbs apricot jelly
For the covering:	
200g/6 oz plain chocolate	6 oz plain chocolate
250ml/8 fl oz hot water	1 cup hot water
150g/5 oz caster sugar	⅔ cup granulated sugar

The Sachertorte is the most famous of all Austrian cakes. It can be left unfilled, or filled with jam. It should be served with whipped cream.
Preheat oven to 160°C/325°F/Gas 3.

Break up the chocolate and melt it over a pan of hot water. Then cool it completely, without letting the chocolate become hard. Beat the butter with the sugar and salt until fluffy, about 5 mins. Add the chocolate and then the egg yolks. Beat until creamy. Whip the egg whites to a stiff snow and stir in the vanilla essence. Slide the egg snow on to the chocolate mixture. Sift over the flour and carefully fold all the ingredients together. Line the bottom of a 24cm/9½ in. cake tin with removable base with greaseproof paper and grease with margarine. Pour in the cake mixture and smooth the top. Bake in the preheated oven on the bottom shelf for 1 hr. 20 mins.

Remove the cake from the oven and leave it to cool in the tin. Then carefully loosen the edge with a knife and invert the cake on to a wire rack. Pull off the paper. Cut the cake in half horizontally. Stir the apricot jam until smooth and brush it over both cut sides of the cake. Place the top layer on the bottom with the jam side uppermost. For the covering, break up the chocolate, add the hot water, and stir until smooth. Add the sugar and simmer for 10 mins. Remove the resulting syrup from the heat and whisk the mixture until it becomes quite thick. Pour the covering over the cake and smooth it flat with a palette knife. Leave to set and serve with whipped cream.

The Sachertorte is a favourite all over the world.

STRAWBERRY CHEESECAKE

Top right, page 107.

Serves 6.

Preparation time without chilling: 1½ hrs.
395 calories/1653 joules

ICED STRAWBERRY GÂTEAU

Centre, pages 106/107.

Serves 8.

Preparation time without freezing: 1 hr. 10 mins.
About 390 calories/1632 joules

Metric/Imperial	American
700ml/1¼ pints vanilla ice cream	3 cups vanilla ice cream
2 sponge bases, ready-baked	2 sponge bases, ready-baked
4x15ml/4 tbs raspberry liqueur or brandy	4 tbs raspberry liqueur or brandy
500g/1 lb strawberries	1 lb strawberries
75g/3 oz caster sugar	⅓ cup granulated sugar
700ml/1¼ pints strawberry ice cream	3 cups strawberry ice cream
375ml/12 fl oz whipping cream	1½ cups whipping cream
3x15ml/3 tbs caster sugar	3 tbs granulated sugar
2½ml/½ tsp vanilla essence	½ tsp vanilla flavoring
12 ratafia biscuits	12 ratafia biscuits

Metric/Imperial	American
For the base:	
250g/8 oz plain flour	2 cups all purpose flour
pinch of salt	pinch of salt
150g/5 oz butter or margarine	⅔ cup butter or margarine
100g/4 oz caster sugar	½ cup granulated sugar
few drops vanilla essence	few drops vanilla flavoring
1 egg	1 egg
For the topping:	
25g/1 oz gelatine	1 oz gelatine
500g/1 lb quark or curd cheese	1 lb quark or curd cheese
1 egg yolk	1 egg yolk
2x15ml/2 tbs strawberry liqueur	2 tbs strawberry liqueur
100g/4 oz caster sugar	½ cup granulated sugar
grated rind ½ lemon	grated rind ½ lemon
375ml/12 fl oz whipping cream	1½ cups whipping cream
300g/10 oz strawberries	2 cups strawberries

Thaw the vanilla ice cream for about 20 mins. until softened. Sprinkle the sponge bases evenly with the raspberry liqueur or brandy. Beat the vanilla ice cream and spread it over 1 sponge base. Freeze for 20 mins.

Hull the strawberries and sprinkle them with sugar. Soften the strawberry ice cream and beat it lightly. Spread it over the vanilla ice cream. Cover with strawberries, reserving a few for decoration. Press the strawberries well into the ice cream and top with the 2nd sponge base. Whip the cream with the sugar and vanilla essence and spoon ⅓ into a piping bag. Cover the top of the gâteau thickly with cream and decorate with swirls of whipped cream and the reserved strawberries. Freeze for a further 2–3 hrs. Before serving, decorate with ratafia biscuits.

Cut the gâteau with a knife dipped in hot water.

NOTE

You can prepare this gâteau with any ice cream of your choice.

Preheat oven to 220°C/425°F/Gas 7.

For the base, sieve the flour and salt into a bowl. Dice the butter or margarine and rub into the flour. Add the sugar and vanilla essence. Make a hollow in the centre, and stir in the beaten egg. Mix together with a knife, and then knead to a smooth dough with your hands. Chill in the refrigerator for 30 mins. Roll out the pastry on a floured board and line a spring-release cake tin with it. Bake it in the preheated oven on the centre shelf for 20 mins. Remove the pastry base from the cake tin and cool it on a wire rack. For the topping, soak the gelatine in a little cold water. Mix the quark with the egg yolk, strawberry liqueur, sugar, and grated lemon rind and stir until smooth. Dissolve the gelatine over a pan of hot water and stir it into the quark mixture. Whip the cream and spoon ⅓ into a piping bag. Fold the remaining cream into the quark mixture. Place the pastry base on a large plate and secure the spring-release ring around it. Spoon in the quark cream, and chill in the refrigerator for 20 mins. Wash and hull the strawberries and halve large fruit. Remove the spring-release ring. Cover the top of the cheesecake with the strawberries and pipe a border of whipped cream around the edge. Chill until serving.

LINZERTORTE

Serves 6.

Preparation time: 1 hr. 25 mins.
About 260 calories/1088 joules

Metric/Imperial	American
200g/6 oz plain flour	1½ cups all purpose flour
200g/6 oz chilled butter	¾ cup chilled butter
100g/4 oz caster sugar	½ cup granulated sugar
pinch of salt	pinch of salt
100g/4 oz ground almonds	1 cup ground almonds
50g/2 oz biscuit crumbs	2 oz biscuit crumbs
grated rind ½ lemon	grated rind ½ lemon
1 egg	1 egg
1x15ml/1 tbs rum	1 tbs rum
For the filling:	
250g/8 oz raspberry jam	½ lb raspberry jelly
milk	milk

Preheat oven to 180°C/350°F/Gas 4.

Sieve the flour into a bowl and rub in the butter. Stir in the sugar, salt, and ground almonds. Add the biscuit crumbs, lemon rind, beaten egg, and rum. Mix well and knead to a smooth dough. Cover and chill in the refrigerator for 30 mins.

Roll out ⅔ of the pastry and line a 24cm/9½ in. flan tin with removable base. Spread the jam thickly over the pastry. Roll our the remaining pastry thinly and cut it into strips about 1cm/½ in. wide. Place the strips over the jam in a lattice pattern. Brush with milk and bake in the preheated oven on the bottom shelf for 1 hr.

Remove the linzertorte from the oven and cool on a wire rack.

HUNYADI GÂTEAU

Serves 8. *Preparation time: 1 hr. 25 mins.*
About 545 calories/2281 joules

Metric/Imperial	American
8 eggs	8 eggs
250g/8 oz caster sugar	1 cup granulated sugar
pinch of salt	pinch of salt
250g/8 oz ground hazelnuts	2 cups ground hazelnuts
100g/4 oz grated chocolate	¼ lb grated chocolate
margarine for greasing	margarine for greasing
500ml/16 fl oz whipping cream	2 cups whipping cream
1x15ml/1 tbs icing sugar	1 tbs confectioners' sugar
150g/5 oz chocolate cake covering	5 oz chocolate cake covering

Preheat oven to 180°C/350°F/Gas 4.

Separate the eggs, and beat the yolks with the sugar and salt until pale and creamy. Fold in the ground hazelnuts. Whip the egg whites to a stiff snow and fold ½ into the hazelnut mixture. Then stir in the grated chocolate and the remaining egg whites. Spoon ⅓ of the mixture into a 24cm/9½ in. greased cake tin with removable base and bake in the preheated oven on the centre shelf for 15 mins.

Cool the base on a wire rack. Bake 2 more bases from the remaining hazelnut mixture and leave them to cool.

For the filling, whip the cream with the sifted icing sugar and spread it over 2 of the cake bases. Place them on top of each other and cover with the 3rd cake. Melt the chocolate cake covering and brush it all over the gâteau. Leave it to set before serving.

The pastry for the Linzertorte contains ground almonds, lemon rind, and rum.

Named after a Hungarian folk hero: Hunyadi gâteau.

STRAWBERRY CREAM ROULADE

Bottom right, page 107.

Serves 8.

Preparation time: 1 hr.
About 190 calories/795 joules

Metric/Imperial	American
6 egg yolks	6 egg yolks
175g/6 oz caster sugar	¾ cup granulated sugar
6 egg whites	6 egg whites
75g/3 oz plain flour	¾ cup all purpose flour
75g/3 oz cornflour	¾ cup cornstarch
1x5ml/1 tsp baking powder	1 tsp double acting baking powder
75g/3 oz ground almonds	¾ cup ground almonds
oil or margarine for greasing	oil or margarine for greasing
For the filling and decoration:	
750g/1½ lbs strawberries	1½ lbs strawberries
50g/2 oz caster sugar	¼ cup granulated sugar
25g/1 oz gelatine	1 oz gelatine
500ml/16 fl oz whipping cream	2 cups whipping cream
2x15ml/2 tbs icing sugar	2 tbs confectioners' sugar
1x15ml/1 tbs pistachio nuts	1 tbs pistachio nuts

Preheat oven to 200°C/400°F/Gas 6.

Beat the egg yolks until pale and creamy and stir in ⅔ of the sugar. Whip the egg whites with the remaining sugar to a firm snow and gently slide them on to the egg yolks. Mix the flour with the cornflour and baking powder and sieve over the egg whites. Sprinkle with ground almonds and, with a metal spoon, very gently mix all the ingredients together.

Line a baking sheet with greaseproof paper and grease with oil or margarine. Spread the batter evenly over the paper and fold up the front edge to prevent the mixture from running off. Bake in the preheated oven on the centre shelf for 15 mins.

Remove from the oven and immediately invert the cake on to a clean tea towel sprinkled with sugar. Brush the paper with cold water and carefully pull it off. With the help of the tea towel, loosely roll up the cake and leave it to cool.

Meanwhile, for the filling, hull and halve the strawberries and sprinkle them with sugar. Set them aside for 15 mins. Soak the gelatine in cold water. Whip the cream and sweeten it with sieved icing sugar. Dissolve the gelatine over a pan of hot water, cool slightly, and stir it into the cream.

Unroll the roulade and spread it with ⅔ of the cream. Reserving a few for decoration, place the strawberries on top of the cream. Roll up the roulade and spread the remaining cream all over it. Pipe a few swirls of cream along the centre and decorate with strawberry halves and pistachio nuts.

STRAWBERRY SLICES *Top left, page 106.*

Makes 10.

Preparation time: 45 mins.
About 350 calories/1465 joules

Metric/Imperial	American
250g/8 oz frozen puff pastry	½ lb frozen puff paste
1 egg yolk	1 egg yolk
500g/1 lb strawberries	1 lb strawberries
100g/4 oz caster sugar	½ cup granulated sugar
375ml/12 fl oz whipping cream	1½ cups whipping cream
4x15ml/4 tbs vanilla sugar	4 tbs vanilla flavored sugar
icing sugar	icing sugar

Preheat oven to 200°C/400°F/Gas 6.

Defrost the puff pastry according to instructions on the packet. Roll it out thinly and cut it into 10 squares. Brush the tops with beaten egg yolk and place on a wetted baking sheet. Bake in the preheated oven on the centre shelf for 25 mins.

Remove the squares from the oven and leave to cool. Slice each one in half horizontally.

For the filling, hull and halve the strawberries and sprinkle them with sugar. Leave to marinade for 10 mins.

Meanwhile, whip the cream and sweeten with vanilla sugar. Drain the strawberries and place them on the bottom halves of the pastry squares. Cover with whipped cream and top with pastry lids. Sprinkle the slices with icing sugar before serving.

STRAWBERRY TARTLETS

Bottom centre, pages 106/107.

Preparation time: 25 mins.
About 190 calories/795 joules

Metric/Imperial	American
500g/1 lb small strawberries	1 lb small strawberries
100g/4 oz caster sugar	½ cup granulated sugar
8 tartlet cases, ready-baked	8 tartlet shells, ready-baked

Wash, hull, and drain the strawberries and sprinkle them with sugar. Stir well, cover, and leave to marinade for 15 mins. Drain the strawberries and pile into the tartlet cases. Serve with vanilla flavoured whipped cream.

CURD CHEESE AND FRUIT GÂTEAU

Serves 8.

Preparation time without chilling: 1 hr. 20 mins.
About 450 calories/1883 joules

Metric/Imperial	American
For the cake:	
4 eggs	4 eggs
4x15ml/4 tbs hot water	4 tbs hot water
100g/4 oz caster sugar	½ cup granulated sugar
2½ml/½ tsp vanilla essence	½ tsp vanilla flavoring
100g/4 oz plain flour	1 cup all purpose flour
75g/3 oz cornflour	¾ cup cornstarch
1x5ml/1 tsp baking powder	1 tsp double acting baking powder
margarine for greasing	margarine for greasing
For the filling:	
25g/1 oz gelatine	1 oz gelatine
2 eggs	2 eggs
300g/10 oz curd cheese	10 oz curd cheese
juice 1 lemon	juice 1 lemon
2x15ml/2 tbs vanilla sugar	2 tbs vanilla flavored sugar
100g/4 oz caster sugar	½ cup granulated sugar
5x15ml/5 tbs milk	5 tbs milk
4x15ml/4 tbs hot water	4 tbs hot water
375ml/12 fl oz whipping cream	1½ cups whipping cream
3 bananas, sliced	3 bananas, sliced
150g/5 oz tinned mandarin oranges	5 oz canned mandarin oranges
250g/8 oz tinned cherries	8 oz canned cherries
For the decoration:	
1x15ml/1 tbs butter	1 tbs butter
75g/3 oz flaked almonds	½ cup flaked almonds
250ml/8 fl oz whipping cream	1 cup whipping cream
2x15ml/2 tbs vanilla sugar	2 tbs vanilla flavored sugar

This curd cheese and fruit gâteau
is filled with cream, cheese, bananas,
mandarin oranges, and cherries.

Preheat oven to 180°C/350°F/Gas 4.

For the cake, separate the eggs and beat the yolks with the water until pale and fluffy. Gradually beat in the sugar and vanilla. Whip the egg whites to a firm snow and slide on to the egg mixture. Mix the plain flour with the cornflour and baking powder, sieve over the egg whites and gently fold in. Line a 24cm/9½ in. cake tin with removable base with greased greaseproof paper and pour in the cake mixture. Smooth the top flat and bake in the preheated oven on the centre shelf for 30 mins. Cool the cake on a wire rack.

For the filling, soak the gelatine in a little cold water. Separate the eggs. Beat the curd cheese with the lemon juice, vanilla and caster sugars, egg yolks and milk until creamy. Dissolve the gelatine in the hot water and beat it into the cheese mixture. Cover and chill the mixture in the refrigerator. In separate bowls, whip the egg whites and cream until stiff. As soon as the cheese mixture begins to set, fold in the egg whites and cream. Cut a thin slice horizontally off the cake and spread ⅓ of the filling over the thicker slice. Cover with the sliced bananas, and the drained mandarin oranges and cherries. Reserve 12 cherries for decoration. Spread the remaining cheese mixture over the fruit and cover it with the thin cake slice. Chill in the refrigerator for 2–3 hrs.

For the decoration, melt the butter and fry the almonds until golden. Leave them to cool. Whip the cream with the vanilla sugar and spoon ⅓ into a piping bag. Cover the top and sides of the gâteau with the remaining cream and sprinkle with the almonds. Pipe swirls of whipped cream round the edge and top each with a cherry.

Pineapple and chocolate slices.

NUT SLICES

Makes 15-20.

Preparation time wihout chilling: 1 hr.
About 180 calories/753 joules

Metric/Imperial	American
For the pastry:	
200g/6 oz plain flour	1½ cups all purpose flour
50g/2 oz cornflour	½ cup cornstarch
1x5ml/1 tsp baking powder	1 tsp double acting baking powder
pinch of salt	pinch of salt
125g/4 oz margarine	½ cup margarine
65g/2½ oz caster sugar	⅓ cup granulated sugar
1x15ml/1 tbs vanilla sugar	1 tbs vanilla flavored sugar
1 egg	1 egg
For the filling:	
50g/2 oz hazelnuts	½ cup hazelnuts
50g/2 oz walnuts	½ cup walnuts
50g/2 oz almonds	½ cup almonds
25g/1 oz sultanas	2 tbs raisins
25g/1 oz mixed peel	2 tbs candied peel
75g/3 oz caster sugar	⅓ cup granulated sugar
grated rind ½ orange	grated rind ½ orange
4x15ml/4 tbs lemon syrup	4 tbs lemon syrup
1x15ml/1 tbs water	1 tbs water
3x15ml/3 tbs orange juice	3 tbs orange juice
2x15ml/2 tbs grand marnier	2 tbs grand marnier
For the icing:	
75g/3 oz icing sugar	½ cup confectioners' sugar
3x15ml/3 tbs lemon juice	3 tbs lemon juice

Preheat oven to 200°C/400°F/Gas 6.

Sift the flour, cornflour, baking powder, and salt into a bowl. Dice the margarine and rub into the flours. Add the caster sugar and the vanilla sugar. Make a hollow in the centre and stir in the beaten egg. Working from the outside inwards, quickly mix to a smooth dough. Cover and chill in the refrigerator for 1 hr.

For the filling, finely grind the nuts and mix them with the sultanas, mixed peel, sugar, orange rind, lemon syrup, water and orange juice.

Roll out the pastry to 2 rectangles, 25x30cm/ 10x12in. Place 1 rectangle on a floured baking sheet and spread the nut mixture evenly over it, leaving a small border all round. Cover the filling with the 2nd pastry rectangle and seal the edges firmly. Prick the top several times with a fork and bake in the preheated oven on the centre shelf for 25 mins. Remove from the oven and prick the top again several times. Sprinkle with the grand marnier. For the icing, mix the sifted icing sugar with the lemon juice and brush it all over the still warm cake. Cut into slices.

PINEAPPLE AND CHOCOLATE SLICES

Preparation time: 1¼ hrs.
524 calories/2193 joules

Metric/Imperial	American
For the cake:	
3 eggs	3 eggs
3x15ml/3 tbs hot water	3 tbs hot water
150g/5 oz caster sugar	½ cup + 2 tbs granulated sugar
2x15ml/2 tbs vanilla sugar	2 tbs vanilla flavored sugar
100g/4 oz plain flour	1 cup all purpose flour
100g/4 oz cornflour	1 cup cornstarch
2x5ml/2 tsp baking powder	2 tsp double acting baking powder
3x15ml/3 tbs cocoa	3 tbs cocoa
3x15ml/3 tbs rum	3 tbs rum
For the butter cream:	
40g/1½ oz custard powder	⅓ cup custard powder
500ml/16 fl oz milk	2 cups milk
50g/2 oz caster sugar	¼ cup granulated sugar
pinch of salt	pinch of salt
250g/8 oz unsalted butter	1 cup sweet butter
150g/5 oz pineapple jam	5 oz pineapple jelly
4 tinned pineapple slices	4 canned pineapple slices
For the topping:	
25g/1 oz butter	2 tbs butter
175g/6 oz icing sugar	1¼ cups confectioners' sugar
25g/1 oz cocoa	2 tbs cocoa
a little hot water	a little hot water
For the decoration:	
3x15ml/3 tbs flaked almonds, toasted	3 tbs flaked almonds, toasted
1x15ml/1 tbs chopped pistachio nuts	1 tbs chopped pistachio nuts

Preheat oven to 200°C/400°F/Gas 6.

Separate the eggs and beat the yolks and water until pale and creamy. Whisk in 125g/4 oz/½ cup of the caster sugar and the vanilla sugar. Whip the egg whites with the remaining sugar until stiff and place them on top of the egg yolk mixture. Mix the flour with the cornflour, baking powder and cocoa and sieve over the egg whites. With a metal spoon, carefully fold in all the ingredients, and add the rum. Line a baking sheet with greaseproof paper and spread with the mixture. Bake in the preheated oven for 15 mins.

Invert the cake on to a wire rack, pull off the paper, and leave to cool.

For the butter cream, mix the custard powder with a little of the milk and bring the remainder to the boil with the sugar and salt. Remove from the heat and stir in the custard powder. Return to the boil, then leave to cool. Stir occasionally to prevent a skin from forming. Beat the butter until fluffy and gradually beat in the cold custard. Finally, whisk in th pineapple jam.

Drain the pineapple and cut it in even-sized pieces. Cut the cake into 3 even-sized strips and cover 1 strip with some of the butter cream. Place ½ of the pineapple pieces on top and cover with a 2nd cake strip. Repeat the process and place the 3rd cake strip on top. For the topping, melt the butter and stir in the sifted icing sugar, cocoa and a little hot water. Brush this icing over the top of the cake. Spread the remainig butter cream evenly over the sides. Sprinkle this with almonds and the top with chopped pistacio nuts.

Nut slices.

Bilberry boats.

BILBERRY BOATS

Makes 8.

Preparation time without chilling: 45 mins.
About 380 calories/1590 joules

Metric/Imperial	American
For the pastry:	
125g/4 oz plain flour	1 cup all purpose flour
pinch of salt	pinch of salt
60g/2½ oz butter or margarine	⅓ cup butter or margarine
60g/2½ oz caster sugar	⅓ cup granulated sugar
2 egg yolks	2 egg yolks
butter or margarine for greasing	butter or margarine for greasing
For the filling:	
250g/8 oz bilberries	2 cups blueberries
60g/2½ oz sugar	⅓ cup sugar
For the decoration:	
250ml/8 fl oz whipping cream	1 cup whipping cream
1x15ml/1 tbs caster sugar	1 tbs granulated sugar
50g/2 oz flaked almonds	½ cup flaked almonds

Preheat oven to 200°C/400°F/Gas 6.

For the pastry, sift the flour and salt into a bowl. Dice the butter and rub into the flour. Add the sugar. Make a hollow in the centre and stir in the beaten egg yolks. Working from the outside inwards, quickly mix to a firm dough. Cover and chill in the refrigerator for 30 mins.

Roll out the pastry and line 8 greased boat-shaped tartlet tins. Bake in the preheated oven on the centre shelf for 15 mins.

Cool the pastry boats on a wire rack. Pick over the bilberries and sprinkle with sugar. Set them aside for 10 mins. Shortly before serving, fill the boats with the bilberries. Whip the cream and sweeten it with the sugar. Spoon into a piping bag and pipe over the bilberries. Sprinkle with flaked almonds.

EASTER PLAIT

Preparation time without rising: 1 hr. 25 mins.
About 855 calories/3579 joules

Metric/Imperial	American
For the dough:	
500g/1 lb plain flour	4 cups all purpose flour
40g/1½ oz fresh yeast	1½ oz compressed fresh yeast
250ml/8 fl oz lukewarm milk	1 cup lukewarm milk

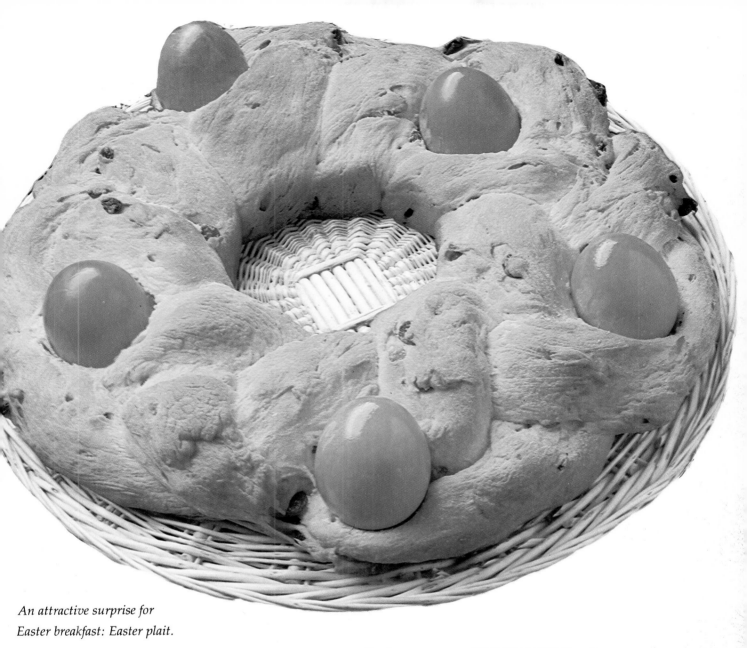

An attractive surprise for
Easter breakfast: Easter plait.

100g/4 oz caster sugar	**½ cup ganulated sugar**
2x15ml/2 tbs vanilla sugar	**2 tbs vanilla flavored sugar**
pinch of salt	**pinch of salt**
1 egg	**1 egg**
100g/4 oz butter or margarine, melted	**½ cup butter or margarine, melted**
150g/5 oz seedless raisins	**1¼ cups stoned raisins**
50g/2 oz mixed peel	**⅓ cup chopped candied peel**
In addition:	
margarine for greasing	**margarine for greasing**
5 empty egg shells, with the contents blown out through small holes pricked in the top and bottom	**5 empty egg shells, with the contents blown out through small holes pricked in the top and bottom**
melted butter	**melted butter**
5 hardboiled eggs, painted red	**5 hardboiled eggs, painted red**

Preheat oven to 200°C/400°F/Gas 6.

For the dough, sift the flour into a bowl and make a hollow in the centre. Crumble the yeast into the hollow and mix it with the milk, a little caster sugar, and some flour drawn in from the sides. Sprinkle with more flour and leave for about 15 mins. in a warm place to rise. Then stir in the remaining caster sugar, vanilla sugar, salt, egg and melted butter or margarine. Knead to a firm dough, and then add the raisins and mixed peel. Beat the dough until it is smooth and elastic. Then leave it to rise again in a warm place for 30 mins.

Roll out the dough to make 3 long, thick sausage shapes. Twist them into a plait. Grease a baking sheet with margarine and place the plait on it, joining the ends together to make a ring. Place the empty egg shells in the holes of the plait, cover with a tea towel, and leave to rise again for 15 mins. Brush the plait with melted butter and bake in the preheated oven on the centre shelf for 45 mins.

Remove the plait from the oven and put it on a plate. Replace the empty egg shells with the red hardboiled eggs.

SAXON CHRISTMAS LOAF

Saxon Christstollen

Preparation time without rising time: 2 hrs. 10 mins.
About 225 calories/941 joules

Metric/Imperial	American
250g/8 oz raisins	2 cups raisins
3x15ml/3 tbs rum	3 tbs rum
500g/1 lb plain flour	4 cups all purpose flour
50g/2 oz fresh yeast	2 oz fresh compressed yeast
100g/4 oz caster sugar	½ cup granulated sugar
125ml/4 fl oz lukewarm milk	½ cup lukewarm milk
2½ml/½ tsp vanilla essence	½ tsp vanilla flavoring
pinch of salt	pinch of salt
200g/6 oz butter, cut in flakes	¾ cup butter, cut in flakes
100g/4 oz chopped mixed peel	¼ lb chopped candied peel
100g/4 oz chopped almonds	¾ cup chopped almonds
margarine for greasing	margarine for greasing
For the topping:	
100g/4 oz butter	½ cup butter
75g/3 oz icing sugar	⅔ cup confectioners' sugar

This traditional German Christmas loaf has been baked in the province of Saxony since the 15th century, and it is now famous all over the world. Preheat oven to 180°C/350°F/Gas 4.

Sprinkle the raisins with rum, cover and leave to soak overnight. Sift the flour into a bowl and make a hollow in the centre. Crumble the yeast into the hollow and sprinkle with 1x5ml/1 tsp of the sugar. Mix with ⅓ of the milk and a little flour drawn in from the sides. Cover and leave to rise for 15 mins. Mix in the flour, remaining sugar, remaining milk, vanilla essence, salt, and flaked butter. Knead well for at least 10 mins. Add the raisins, mixed peel, and almonds. Cover the bowl with a tea towel and leave the dough to rise for 1 hr. Roll out the dough to an oblong about 30cm/12 in. long. Fold over ⅓ of the long side to make the traditional stollen shape. Place on a greased baking sheet and leave it to rise again for 1 hr. Melt the butter and brush ½ over the stollen. Bake in the preheated oven on the centre shelf for 1 hr.

Remove the baked stollen from the oven and brush with the remaining melted butter. Leave to soak in a little and then dust thickly with sieved icing sugar. Wrap the stollen in aluminium foil and leave it to mature for at least 2 weeks before eating.

Saxon Christmas loaf.

EASTER CAKE

Preparation time: 1½ hrs.
About 415 calories/1737 joules

Metric/Imperial	American
For the cake:	
100g/4 oz milk chocolate	¼ lb milk chocolate
100g/4 oz plain chocolate	¼ lb plain chocolate
125ml/4 fl oz single cream	½ cup light cream
100g/4 oz butter or margarine	½ cup butter or margarine
6 eggs	6 eggs
100g/4 oz caster sugar	½ cup granulated sugar
200g/8 oz ground almonds	2 cups ground almonds
200g/8 oz breadcrumbs	½ lb breadcrumbs
grated rind 1 orange and 1 lemon	grated rind 1 orange and 1 lemon
margarine for greasing	margarine for greasing
For the icing:	
150g/5 oz icing sugar	1 cup confectioners' sugar
1x15ml/1 tbs hot water	1 tbs hot water
2x15ml/2 tbs warmed rum	2 tbs warmed rum

Preheat oven to 130°C/275°F/Gas 1.

For this Easter cake you will need a rabbit-shaped biscuit cutter. Break the milk and plain chocolate into a bowl and pour in the cream. Over a pan of hot water, carefully melt the chocolate, stirring continuously. Add the butter or margarine and stir until smooth. Cool slightly. Separate the eggs. Mix the chocolate mixture with the yolks, sugar, ground almonds, breadcrumbs, and orange and lemon rind. Whip the egg whites to a stiff snow and fold into the mixture. Grease a large (26cm/10 in.) cake tin with removable base, and spread with the cake mixture. Bake in the preheated oven on the bottom shelf for 1 hr.

Remove the cake from the oven and cool it on a wire rack.

For the icing, stir the sieved icing sugar with the water and rum until smooth. Place the rabbit biscuit cutter in the centre of the cake and brush all round it with the icing. Remove the biscuit cutter before serving.

NUREMBERG GINGERBREAD

Nurnberger Elisenlebkuchen

Makes 34 pieces.

Preparation time: 45 mins.
About 125 calories/523 joules

Nuremberg gingerbread.

Metric/Imperial	American
3 eggs	3 eggs
250g/8 oz caster sugar	1 cup granulated sugar
2x15ml/2 tbs vanilla sugar	2 tbs vanilla flavored sugar
3x15ml/3 tbs cornflour	3 tbs cornstarch
3x15ml/3 tbs plain flour	3 tbs all purpose flour
1¼ml/¼ tsp baking powder	¼ tsp double acting baking powder
1¼ml/¼ tsp ground cloves	¼ tsp ground cloves
1¼ml/¼ tsp ground ginger	¼ tsp ground ginger
1¼ml/¼ tsp ground cinnamon	¼ tsp ground cinnamon
1¼ml/¼ tsp ground nutmeg	¼ tsp ground nutmeg
1¼ml/¼ tsp ground allspice	¼ tsp ground allspice
1x15ml/1 tbs rum	1 tbs rum
75g/3 oz chopped mixed peel	3 oz chopped candied peel
100g/4 oz ground almonds	1 cup ground almonds
100g/4 oz ground hazelnuts	1 cup ground hazelnuts
34 ricepaper wafers (7cm/3 in.)	34 ricepaper wafers (3 in.)
For the white icing:	
75g/3 oz icing sugar	⅔ cup confectioners' sugar
1x15ml/1 tbs hot water	1 tbs hot water
For the chocolate icing:	
100g/4 oz chocolate cake covering	¼ lb chocolate cake covering

For the decoration:

25g/1 oz almonds	1 oz almonds
25g/1 oz sugar crystals	1 oz sugar crystals

Preheat oven to 150°C/300°F/Gas 2.

Beat the eggs until light and fluffy and gradually add the sugars. Beat until the mixture is very creamy. Stir in the cornflour, flour, baking powder, spice, rum, mixed peel, and the ground almonds and hazelnuts. Mix well. Place about 1x15ml/1 tbs of the mixture on to each wafer and bake on a baking sheet in the preheated oven for 25 mins.

Meanwhile, for the icings, mix the sifted icing sugar with the hot water, and melt the cake covering over a pan of hot water.

Cool the baked gingerbread on a wire rack and ice ½ with the white icing and ½ with the chocolate icing. Decorate the latter with whole almonds, and sprinkle sugar crystals over the white icing.

NOTE

This gingerbread is traditionally served at Christmas.

WITCH'S HOUSE

First cut out the end walls.

Cut strips for a chimney and a fence from the trimmings

*The front end wall has a door and a window cut out.
The 4 walls are stuck together with icing.*

Metric/Imperial	American
For the gingerbread dough:	
250g/8 oz sugar	1 cup sugar
pinch of salt	pinch of salt
750g/1½ lbs honey	1½ lbs honey
100g/4 oz lard	½ cup lard
1¼kgs/2½ lbs plain flour	2½ lbs all purpose flour
250g/8 oz ground almonds	2 cups ground almonds
2x5ml/2 tsp mixed spice	2 tsp mixed spice
3x5ml/3 tsp ground cinnamon	3 tsp ground cinnamon
2 eggs	2 eggs
1x15ml/1 tbs carbonate of ammonia (available at a chemist)	1 tbs carbonate of ammonia (available at pharmacists')
3x5ml/3 tsp water	3 tsp water
For the icing:	
500g/1 lb icing sugar	1 lb confectioners' sugar
4 egg whites	4 egg whites
4x15ml/4 tbs lemon juice	4 tbs lemon juice
For the decoration:	
small sweets like smarties, sugared almonds, jelly beans, biscuits etc.	small sweets like smarties, sugared almonds, jelly beans, biscuits, etc.
icing sugar	icing sugar

If you know the fairy tale of Hansel and Gretel, you will remember the witch's house which was made of gingerbread. This is a traditional Christmas treat for children all over Germany. It takes a great deal of time to prepare, but is well worth the effort.

Preheat the oven to 180°C/350°F/Gas 4.

To make the dough: heat the sugar, salt, honey, and lard and stir until the sugar is dissolved. Leave to cool.

Sift the flour into a bowl and add the ground almonds, spices, honey mixture, and eggs. Mix the carbonate of ammonia with a little cold water and add to the bowl. Mix all the ingredients together and then knead the dough until it is smooth and elastic. Leave it to rest for 30 mins. On a floured work surface, thinly roll out the dough and cut out the shapes for the house:

2 end walls, 19cm/7½ in. wide, 5cm/2 in. high at sides, 24cm/9½ in. high to top.

Leave one wall as it is, and cut a door and a window in the other.

2 side walls, 19cm/7½ in. wide, 5cm/2 in. high.

2 roof pieces, 25cm/10 in. square.

From the trimmings, cut a chimney and a fence. You can also cut figures, trees, and anything else that you feel is relevant.

Place the dough pieces on oiled baking sheets and bake in the preheated oven on the centre shelf for 15 mins. each.

Cool the pieces on a wire rack making sure that they lie absolutely flat. Make the icing by mixing together the sifted icing sugar, egg whites, and lemon juice, and keep it covered with a damp cloth while working with each portion. Have ready the sweets for the decoration. Spread each sweet with a little icing and stick it to the flat cut-outs. Leave to dry, preferably overnight. To assemble the house, have a bread board or strong cardboard on which to make it, ready. The house is stuck together with icing, so you will need a great deal of patience. Smear some icing along the edges of the walls and join them together. Use a jar or something similar to prop them up while they dry. Spread some icing along the upper edges of the walls and 1 edge of the roof pieces and fasten the roof to the walls. Stick the chimney on to the roof. Stick any remaining sweets wherever you find a space, and make the fence. Finally, dust the house with icing sugar to make it look as though it is covered in snow.

NOTE
If you have by spare dough, roll out a base plate to use instead of the breadboard or cardboard, and cover with icing.

Completely edible: witch's house.

FATHER CHRISTMAS BISCUIT

Preparation time without resting: 1½ hrs.
About 4365 calories/18271 joules
for the Father Christmas
About 130 calories/544 joules for each biscuit

Metric/Imperial	American
For the dough:	
375g/12 oz chopped almonds	2½ cups chopped almonds
750g/1½ lbs sugar	1½ lbs sugar
750g/1½ lbs honey	1½ lbs honey
250g/8 oz chopped mixed peel	½ lb chopped candied peel
1x5ml/1 tsp mixed spice	1 tsp mixed spice
25g/1 oz ground cinnamon	2 tbs ground cinnamon
800g/1¾ lbs plain flour	1¾ lbs all purpose flour
1x15ml/1 tbs bicarbonate of soda	1 tbs bicarbonate of soda
For the icing:	
200g/6 oz icing sugar	1¼ cups confectioners' sugar
1 egg white	1 egg white
1x15ml/1 tbs lemon juice	1 tbs lemon juice

Preheat oven to 200°C/400°F/Gas 6.
For the dough, cook the almonds, sugar, and honey for 10 mins. until golden. Add the mixed peel and spices. Pour into a mixing bowl and leave to cool. Stir in the sifted flour and bicarbonate of soda and knead to a smooth dough. Dust a baking sheet lightly with flour and roll out the dough on it. Leave it to rest overnight. Bake in the preheated oven on the centre shelf for 40 mins.

In the meantime, cut a Father Christmas shape (around 30x12cm/12x5in.) out of a piece of cardboard. Remove the baking sheet from the oven and, using the cardboard template as a guide, cut out the Father Christmas. (Cut the trimmings into biscuits and decorate as you like.)

For the icing, mix the sifted icing sugar with the egg white and add the lemon juice in drops. The mixture must be of piping consistency. Spoon the icing into a piping bag and pipe the outer edges, face, hat, and clothes of the Father Christmas on to the cut-out. Leave it to dry.

Gingerbread hearts are coated with chocolate.

GINGERBREAD HEARTS

Makes 90.

Preparation time: 1 hr. 35 mins.
About 100 calories/418 joules

Metric/Imperial	American
For the dough:	
500g/1 lb honey	1 lb honey
250g/8 oz sugar	1 cup sugar
100g/4 oz butter	½ cup butter
2 eggs, salt	2 eggs, salt
60g/2½ oz chopped mixed peel	2½ oz chopped candied peel
2x5ml/2 tsp ground cinnamon	2 tsp ground cinnamon
1x5ml/1 tsp mixed spice	1 tsp mixed spice
1kg/2¼ lbs plain flour	2¼ lbs all purpose flour
2x15ml/2 tbs baking powder	2 tbs double acting baking powder
margarine for greasing	margarine for greasing
For the icing:	
200g/6 oz plain chocolate	6 oz plain chocolate
25g/1 oz butter	2 tbs butter

Preheat oven to 200°C/400°F/Gas 6.
Bring the honey with the sugar and butter to the boil, remove from the heat, and stir until lukewarm.

Lightly beat the eggs and add to the mixture with the salt, mixed peel, spice, and sifted flour mixed with baking powder. Knead well, and then roll out the dough thickly. Cut out heart shapes with a biscuit cutter and place on a greased baking sheet. Bake in the preheated oven on the centre shelf for 15 mins.

Carefully remove the hearts from the baking sheet and cool on a wire rack.

For the icing, melt the chocolate over a pan of hot water. Stir in the butter and remove from the heat. Stir until the mixture is of a spreading consistency, then coat the hearts.

BURNT ALMONDS

Preparation time: 50 mins.
About 13 calories/54 joules

Metric/Imperial	American
500g/1 lb unskinned almonds	**1 lb unskinned almonds**
500g/1 lb sugar	**1 lb sugar**
250ml/8 fl oz water	**1 cup water**
1x5ml/1 tsp ground cinnamon	**1 tsp ground cinnamon**
125ml/4 fl oz rose water	**½ cup rose water**
oil for greasing	**oil for greasing**

Preheat oven to 200°C/400°F/Gas 6.

Rub the almonds with a dry cloth. Bring the sugar and water to the boil and add the cinnamon. Stir in the almonds and simmer for 20 mins. Cool for 1 min. then pour in the rose water. Return to the heat and cook until the sugar is completely dissolved and sticks to the almonds. This will take about 5 mins. Line 2 baking sheets with greased aluminium foil. Pour the almonds on to the foil and separate them very quickly with two forks. Place the baking trays in the preheated oven for 5 mins. to glaze the almonds.   Remove the almonds from the oven and leave to cool.

NOTE
Should the sugar crust fall off the almonds, bring the sugar to the boil with 2x15ml/2 tbs water and repeat the process.

STUFFED DATES

Preparation time: 25 mins.
Altogether about 2725 calories/11405 joules

Metric/Imperial	American
250g/½ lb dates	**½ lb dates**
100g/4 oz whole almonds	**⅔ cup whole almonds**
200g/6 oz almond paste	**6 oz almond paste**
100g/4 oz plain chocolate cake covering	**¼ lb plain chocolate cake covering**

For anyone with a sweet tooth, these stuffed dates are a treat.

Split the dates open lengthwise and remove the stones. Place an almond inside each date. Thinly roll out the almond paste and cut it into squares. Wrap these around the stuffed dates. Melt the chocolate cake covering according to instructions on the packet, and dip the dates in it to cover half of each one. Dry them on a wire rack.

STUFFED WALNUTS

Makes 20.

Preparation time: 30 mins.
About 85 calories/356 joules

Metric/Imperial	American
50g/2 oz plain chocolate	**2 oz plain chocolate**
50g/2 oz ground almonds	**½ cup ground almonds**
40 large walnut halves	**40 large walnut halves**
150g/5 oz sugar	**⅔ cup sugar**

Melt the chocolate and stir in the ground almonds. Leave the mixture to cool, and then shape it into balls. Place these between 2 walnut halves and spear them on to wooden cocktail sticks. Bring the sugar to the boil and simmer until it turns a rich golden brown. Dip the stuffed walnuts into the caramel and leave them to dry.

Burnt almonds.

DANISH CHRISTMAS CUP

Serves 6.

Metric/Imperial	American
1 orange	1 orange
12 cubes of sugar	12 cubes of sugar
2 litres red wine	2 litres red wine
5cm/2 in. cinnamon stick	2 in. cinnamon stick
pinch of grated nutmeg	pinch of grated nutmeg
450g/1 lb tinned cherries, stoned	1 lb canned cherries, stoned
5x15ml/5 tbs kirsch	5 tbs kirsch

This traditional Danish wine cup is served cold, but it should warm you nevertheless.
Wash the orange in hot water and rub the sugar cubes all over the orange peel to extract the oil. Heat the sugar, red wine, cinnamon stick, and nutmeg until foaming. Leave to cool. Add the cherries with their juice and the kirsch. Cover and chill for at least 2 hrs. Remove the cinnamon stick and serve in a large glass bowl.

A traditional Danish Christmas cup.

IRISH COFFEE

Metric/Imperial	American
250ml/8 fl oz double cream	1 cup heavy cream
750ml/27 fl oz water	3½ cups water
75g/3 oz ground coffee	6 tbs ground coffee
8x5ml/8 tsp brown sugar	8 tsp brown sugar
4 measures Irish whiskey	4 measures Irish whiskey

Irish coffee, the world famous after-dinner drink, must always be made with Irish whiskey. It is served in heatproof glasses. Experts are divided over the correct way of preparing Irish coffee. Here is 1 method.
Chill the cream. Bring the water to the boil. Place the coffee in a jug and pour over the boiling water. Leave for 5 mins.
Place 2x5ml/2 tsp of sugar in each glass and fill it ¾ full with hot coffee. Stir until the sugar has dissolved. Add the whiskey and top with the cream. Do not stir.

WHITE WINE CUP

Serves 6–8.

Metric/Imperial	American
500g/1 lb fresh strawberries or peaches	1 lb fresh strawberries or peaches
75g/3 oz caster sugar	⅓ cup granulated sugar
rind 1 lemon	rind 1 lemon
2 bottles Rhine wine	2 bottles Rhine wine
1 bottle Moselle wine	1 bottle Moselle wine
1 bottle sparkling wine	1 bottle sparkling wine

Wash and hull the strawberries or skin, stone, and slice the peaches. Place the fruit in a large glass bowl and sprinkle with sugar. Peel the lemon in one long twist and hang this into the bowl. Pour in one bottle of Rhine wine, cover, and chill for 1 hr.
Remove the lemon peel and pour in the remaining still wine. Just before serving, add the sparkling wine.

NOTE
White wine cup can be made with any fresh or preserved fruit.

White wine cup.

ICED COFFEE

Metric/Imperial	American
125ml/4 fl oz whipping cream	½ cup whipping cream
vanilla ice cream	vanilla ice cream
500ml/16 fl oz strong, chilled coffee	2 cups strong, chilled coffee
sugar to taste	sugar to taste
1x15ml/1 tbs grated chocolate	1 tbs grated chocolate
4 fan wafers	4 fan wafers

Whip the cream, spoon it into a piping bag and chill in the refrigerator. Place 2 scoops of ice cream into each of 4 glasses. Pour over the sweetened coffee and decorate with a large swirl of whipped cream. Sprinkle with grated chocolate and serve with fan wafers and a drinking straw.

Iced coffee.

Iced tea.

ICED TEA

Serves 8.

Metric/Imperial	American
6x5ml/6 tsp tea leaves	6 tsp tea leaves
500ml/16 fl oz boiling water	2 cups boiling water
juice 1 lemon	juice 1 lemon
2x15ml/2 tbs orange syrup	2 tbs orange syrup
sugar to taste	sugar to taste
ice cubes	ice cubes
8 measures rum	8 measures rum
1 lemon	1 lemon

Place the tea leaves in a heated tea pot and pour the boiling water over. Leave to stand for 5 mins. Strain the tea and add the lemon juice and orange syrup. Sweeten to taste. Place plenty of ice cubes in 8 tall glasses, and pour 1 measure of rum into each. Fill the glasses with the hot tea and garnish each with a slice of lemon.

BLACK RUSSIAN

Serves 1.

1 measure kahlúa or tia maria
2 measures vodka

Mix the Kahlúa or tia maria with the vodka and serve on the rocks.

GLÖGG

Swedish Christmas punch

Serves 8.

Metric/Imperial	American
1 litre red wine	1 litre red wine
1 bottle sweet muscat wine	1 bottle sweet muscat wine
250ml/8 fl oz white vermouth	1 cup white vermouth
1x15ml/1 tbs angostura bitters	1 tbs angostura bitters
100g/4 oz raisins	1 cup raisins
grated rind 2 oranges	grated rind 2 oranges
6 crushed cardamom pods	6 crushed cardamom pods
5 cloves	5 cloves
1 piece of preserved stem ginger, chopped	1 piece of preserved stem ginger, chopped
½ cinnamon stick, crumbled	½ cinnamon stick, crumbled
175ml/3 fl oz aquavit or vodka	⅓ cup aquavit or vodka
150g/5 oz sugar	⅔ cup sugar
100g/4 oz whole almonds	¾ cup whole almonds

Flaming punch.

Combine the red wine, sweet wine, vermouth, angostura bitters, raisins, orange rind, cardamom, cloves, chopped ginger, and crumbled cinnamon in a large enamelled saucepan. Stir the mixture, cover it, and leave overnight. Just before serving, stir in the aquavit or vodka, sugar, and almonds, and bring the punch to the boil. Remove it from the heat and serve hot.

FLAMING PUNCH

Feuerzangen Bowle

Preparation time: 10 mins.

Metric/Imperial	American
2 bottles of red wine	2 bottles of red wine
4 cloves	4 cloves
piece of orange rind	piece of orange rind
1 piece of cinnamon stick	1 piece of cinnamon stick
juice 1 lemon	juice 1 lemon
1 sugar cone of 250g/8 oz	1 sugar cone of ½ lb
500ml/1 pint of dark rum	2½ cups of dark rum

The Feuerzangen Bowle is a very potent traditional German punch served on New Year's Eve. It is really superb. It might be difficult to obtain the required sugar cone, but if you find one when travelling abroad take it home and serve this delicious party piece. A large piece of loaf sugar could be substituted for the sugar cone.

To prepare the punch you will need some metal ice tongs, a ovenproof bowl and a table top burner. Pour the wine into the bowl, spike the orange rind with the cloves and add to the wine with the cinnamon and lemon juice. Heat on the burner until hot but not boiling. Place the ice tongs across the top of the bowl and lay the sugar cone on it with the pointed end to the handle of the tongs so that the melting sugar drips into the bowl. Pour enough rum over the sugar to completely soak it. Ignite and leave to burn. Switch off the room lights for greatest effect. Keep adding rum to the sugar to maintain the flame and enable the sugar to melt into the wine. When all the sugar has melted and the flames have died down, the punch is ready to be drunk. Serve the hot punch with various sweet and savoury biscuits or nuts.